M000312335

Second Edition

World Link

Developing English Fluency

Susan Stempleski
James R. Morgan
Nancy Douglas

3

HEINLE
CENGAGE Learning™

Australia • Brazil • Japan • Korea • Mexico • Singapore • Spain • United Kingdom • United States

HEINLE
CENGAGE Learning™

World Link 3: Developing English Fluency
2nd Edition

Susan Stempleski
James R. Morgan
Nancy Douglas

Publisher: Sherrise Roehr
Senior Development Editor:
Jennifer Meldrum
Senior Development Editor:
Katherine Carroll
Director of Global Marketing:
Ian Martin
Senior Product Marketing Manager:
Katie Kelley
Assistant Marketing Manager:
Anders Bylund
Content Project Manager:
John Sarantakis
Senior Print Buyer:
Mary Beth Hennebury
Composition: Bill Smith Group
Cover/Text Design: Page2 LLC
Cover Image: iStockphoto

© 2011, 2005, Heinle Cengage Learning

ALL RIGHTS RESERVED. No part of this work covered by the copyright herein may be reproduced, transmitted, stored or used in any form or by any means graphic, electronic, or mechanical, including but not limited to photocopying, recording, scanning, digitizing, taping, Web distribution, information networks, or information storage and retrieval systems, except as permitted under Section 107 or 108 of the 1976 United States Copyright Act, without the prior written permission of the publisher.

For permission to use material from this text or product,
submit all requests online at **www.cengage.com/permissions**
Further permissions questions can be emailed to
permissionrequest@cengage.com

Library of Congress Control Number: 2009939402
Student Book:
ISBN-13: 978-1-4240-5503-6
ISBN-10: 1-4240-5503-2
Student Book with Student CD-ROM:
ISBN-13: 978-1-4240-6820-3
ISBN-10: 1-4240-6820-7

Heinle
20 Channel Center Street
Boston, MA 02210
USA

Cengage learning is a leading provider of customized learning solutions with office locations around the globe, including Singapore, the United Kingdom, Australia, Mexico, Brazil, and Japan. Locate our local office at:
international.cengage.com/region

Cengage Learning products are represented in Canada by Nelson Education, Ltd.

Visit Heinle online at **elt.heinle.com**
Visit our corporate website at **cengage.com**

Photo Credits: 2: Tomas Bercic/istockphoto **4:** Bruce Laurance/Photographer's Choice /Getty images **7:** top right image copyright Losevsky Pavel 2009 / Used under license from Shutterstock.com, center left Purestock/Jupiter Images, center right image copyright Andresr/used under license from www.shutterstock.com, bottom left Hill Street Studios/Blend Images/Jupiter Images, bottom right image copyright Supri Suharjoto/used under license from www.shutterstock.com **8:** top right Image Copyright Mircea BEZERGHEANU 2009/Used under the license of Shutterstock.com, center right Library of Congress **9:** top right Dennis Morris/iStockphoto.com, center right Susan Trigg/iStockphoto.com, bottom left mcswin /iStockphoto.com **11:** top left Poelzer Wolfgang / Alamy, top center image copyright Steven Lee/Used under license from Shutterstock.com, top right Luciano Mortula/iStockphoto.com, center left oversnap/iStockphoto.com, center right image copyright Yui 2009/Used under license from Shutterstock.com, **12:** image copyright Golden Pixels LLC 2009 / Used under license from Shutterstock.com **13:** center right copyright 2005 PhotoDisc Inc., bottom right copyright 2005 PhotoDisc Inc., top right image copyright Nowik/used under license from www.shutterstock.com **17:** Image Copyright Rolf Meinow 2010/used under license from www.shutterstock.com **18:** tr image copyright Andrey Arkusha 2010/used under license from www.shutterstock.com **18:** br image copyright Kovalev Sergey/Used under license from www.shutterstock.com **19:** all images copyright 2005 PhotoDisc Inc. **21:** center right AtnoYdur/iStockphoto.com, center left image copyright Yuri Arcurs 2009/Used under license from Shutterstock.Com **22:** top left Ryan McVay/Photodisc/Jupiter Images, top right Jack Hollingsworth /Blend Images/Jupiter Images, center left Francisco Romero/iStockphoto.com, center right Image copyright Monkey Business Images 2009/Used under license from Shutterstock.com **26:** center right Andersen Ross/Stockbyte/Jupiter Images, bottom right image copyright Dmitriy Shironosov 2009/ Used under license from Shutterstock.com **29:** top right Carolina Garcia Aranda/Dreamstime.com, bottom right copyright 2005 PhotoDisc Inc. **33:** Jacob Wackerhausen/iStockphoto.com **36:** top right Used under license from Shutterstock.Com, bottom center Image copyright Anastasia Bobrova 2009/Used under license from Shutterstock.com, center right ALEAIMAGE/iStockphoto.com, bottom left image copyright Jose Gil 2009/Used under license from shutterstock, bottom right image copyright Kitti 2009/Used under license from shutterstock **37:** Aldo Murillo/iStockphoto.com **38:** bottom left Image copyright Darren Hubley 2009/Used under license from Shutterstock.com, bottom center image copyright hunta 2009/ Used under license from Shutterstock.com, bottom center image copyright Liudmila P. Sundikova 2009/ Used under license from Shutterstock.com, bottom right PHANIE / Photo Researchers Inc. **40:** bottom right George Marks/Retrofile /Getty Images, bottom left Joselito Briones/iStockphoto.com **42:** top center Joseph C. Justice Jr./iStockphoto.com, top right Juanmonino/iStockphoto.com, top right image copyright Yuri Arcurs 2009/Used under license from Shutterstock.com **43:** top right Image copyright CREATISTA 2009/Used under license from Shutterstock.com, center left image copyright Solid Web Designs LTD 2008/ Used under license from Shutterstock.com, center right Jamie Carroll/iStockphoto.com, bottom left image copyright R McKown2009/ Used under license from Shutterstock.com, Bottom right image copyright Phil Date2009/ Used under license from Shutterstock.com **46:** center Image copyright Evok20 2009/Used under license from Shutterstock.com, bottom right image copyright Monkey Business Images 2009/Used under license from Shutterstock.com Page 47 center right Tombaky /iStockphoto.com, bottom right image copyright Max romeo 2009/ Used under license from Shutterstock.com **48:** bottom left image copyright Arteki 2008/Used under license from Shutterstock.com, bottom right image copyright HLPhoto 2009/Used under license from Shutterstock.com **51:** image copyright Peter Baxter 2009/Used under license from Shutterstock.com **52:** center right image

Printed in the United States of America
1 2 3 4 5 6 7 8 9 10 - 14 13 12 11 10

Acknowledgments

Thank you to the educators who provided invaluable feedback throughout the development of the second edition of the *World Link* series: Rocio Abarca, Instituto Tecnológico de Costa Rica / FUNDATEC; Anthony Acevedo, ICPNA (Instituto Cultural Peruano Norteamericano); David Aduviri, CBA (Centro Boliviano Americano) - La Paz; Ramon Aguilar, Universidad Tecnológica de Hermosillo; Miguel Arrazola, CBA (Centro Boliviano Americano) - Santa Cruz; Cecilia Avila, Universidad de Xalapa; Isabel Baracat, CCI (Centro de Comunicação Inglesa); Andrea Brotto, CEICOM (Centro de Idiomas para Comunidades); George Bozanich, Soongsil University; Emma Campo, Universidad Central; Martha Carrasco, Universidad Autonoma de Sinaloa; Herbert Chavel, Korea Advanced Institute of Science and Technology; Denise de Bartolomeo, AMICANA (Asociación Mendocina de Intercambio Cultural Argentino Norteamericano); Rodrigo de Campos Rezende, SEVEN Idiomas; John Dennis, Hokuriku University; Kirvin Andrew Dyer, Yan Ping High School; Daniela Frillochi, ARICANA (Asociación Rosarina de Intercambio Cultural Argentino Norteamericano); Jose Gonzales, ICPNA (Instituto Cultural Peruano Norteamericano); Marina Gonzalez, Instituto Universitario de Lenguas Modernas; Robert Gordon, Korea Advanced Institute of Science and Technology; Gu Yingruo, Research Institute of Xiangzhou District, ZhuHai; Yo-Tien Ho, Takming University; Roxana Jimenez, Instituto Tecnológico de Costa Rica / FUNDATEC; Sirina Kainongsuang, Perfect Publishing Company Limited; Karen Ko, ChinYi University; Ching-Hua Lin, National Taiwan University of Science and Technology; Simon Liu, ChinYi University; Maria Helena Luna, Tronwell; Ady Marrero, Alianza Cultural Uruguay Estados Unidos; Nancy Mcaleer, ELC Universidad Interamericana de Panama; Michael McCallister, Feng Chia University Language Center; José Antonio Mendes Lopes, ICBEU (Instituto Cultural Brasil Estados Unidos); Leonardo Mercado, ICPNA (Instituto Cultural Peruano Norteamericano); Tania Molina, Instituto Tecnológico de Costa Rica / FUNDATEC; Iliana Mora, Instituto Tecnológico de Costa Rica / FUNDATEC; Fernando Morales, Universidad Tecnológica de Hermosillo; Vivian Morghen, ICANA (Instituto Cultural Argentino Norteamericano); Niu Yuchun, New Oriental School Beijing; Elizabeth Ortiz, COPEI (Copol English Institute); Virginia Ortiz, Universidad Autonoma de Tamaulipas; Peter Reilly, Universidad Bonaterra; Ren Huijun, New Oriental School Hangzhou; Andreina Romero, URBE (Universidad Rafael Belloso Chacín); Adelina Ruiz, Instituto Tecnologico de Estudios Superiores de Occidente; Eleonora Salas, IICANA (Instituto de Intercambio Cultural Argentino Norteamericano); Mary Sarawit, Naresuan University International College; Jenay Seymour, Hong-ik University; Huang Shuang, Shanghai International Studies University; Sávio Siqueira, ACBEU (Asociação Cultural Brasil Estados Unidos) / UFBA (Universidade Federal da Bahia); Beatriz Solina, ARICANA (Asociación Rosarina de Intercambio Cultural Argentino Norteamericano); Tran Nguyen Hoai Chi, Vietnam USA Society English Training Service Center; Maria Inés Valsecchi, Universidad Nacional de Río Cuarto; Patricia Veciño, ICANA (Instituto Cultural Argentino Norteamericano); Punchalee Wasanasomsithi, Chulalongkorn University; Tomoe Watanabe, Hiroshima City University; Tomohiro Yanagi, Chubu University; Jia Yuan, Global IELTS School.

(Photo credit continued from copyright page) copyright Hypestock 2009/Used under license from Shutterstock.com, center Brian Pamphilon/iStockphoto.com **55:** top left Arpad Benedek/IStockphoto.com, top right anouchka/iStockphoto.com, bottom left Derek Latta/iStockphoto.com, bottom right image copyright Kim Ruoff 2009/ Used under license from Shutterstock.com **57:** image copyright Tara Flake 2009/Used under license from Shutterstock.com **59:** image copyright EuToch 2009/Used under license from Shutterstock.com **60:** top left Jon Helgason/klikk, iStockphoto.com, center left Image copyright Dennis Ku 2009/Used under license from Shutterstock.com, center right John Pitcher/iStockphoto.com, top right Catharina van den Dikkenberg/toos/iStockphoto.com. **64:** top right image copyright Eduard Stelmakh 2009/ Used under license from Shutterstock.com, center right image copyright Monkey Business Images 2009/ Used under license from Shutterstock.com, top right image copyright James Steidl/used under license from www.shutterstock.com, center image copyright mypokcik/used under license from www.shutterstock.com, center right image copyright Steve Collender/used under license from www.shutterstock.com **69:** top left Photos.com, top right Nick M. Do/iStockphoto.com, center left Valua Vitaly/iStockphoto.com **70:** top image copyright Orange Line Media 2009/Used under license from Shutterstock.com, center image copyright Edwin Verin 2009/Used under license from Shutterstock.Com, bottom image copyright Liz Van Steenburgh 2009/Used under license from Shutterstock.Com **72:** left MorePixels/iStockphoto.com, right Peter Dazeley/Photographer's Choice/Getty Images **73:** left Sharon Dominick/iStockphoto.com, center iStockphoto.com, right image copyright Jaimie Duplass 2009 / Used under license from Shutterstock.com **74:** left Justin Horrocks/iStockphoto.com, center kristian sekulic/iStockphoto.com, right Alanpoulson/Dreamstime.com **75:** top image copyright Christopher Futcher 2009/Used under license from Shutterstock.Com, center image copyright Dave Thompson 2009/Used under license from Shutterstock.com, bottom © Elena Elisseeva | Dreamstime.com **76:** Christopher Futcher| Dreamstime.com **79:** Ariel Skelley/CORBIS **80:** right © Lidps | Dreamstime.com, left Noah Clayton/Digital Vision/Jupiter Images **82:** top Lance Bellers/iStockphoto.com, center Steven Dern/iStockphoto.com, bottom Comstock/Jupiterimages **83:** image copyright nadja_tj 2010/used under license from www.shutterstock.com **85:** Drive Images / Alamy **87:** top image copyright Samot 2009/ Used under license from Shutterstock.com, bottom Inc Greer & Associates/Superstock/PhotoLibrary **89:** Sean Nel/iStockphoto.com **88:** center AP Photo/John Marshall, bottom Jacom Stephens/iStockphoto.com **90:** left Radius Images/Jupiter images, right image copyright R. Gino Santa Maria/used under license from www.shutterstock.com **92:** Robert Landau / Alamy **91:** image copyright Robert Adrian Hillman 2010/used under license from www.shutterstock.com **95:** image copyright iofoto 2010/Used under license from Shutterstock.com **96:** top left image copyright atanas.dk 2010/Used under license from Shutterstock.com, top right image copyright Steve Rosset 2010/Used under license from Shutterstock.com, center image copyright Solaria 2010/Used under license from Shutterstock.com, center left image copyright funflow 2010/used under license from www.shutterstock.com, center right image copyright Jane September 2010/used under license from www.shutterstock.com **97:** right Aldo Murillo/iStockphoto.com, left Alexander Podshivalov/iStockphoto.com **98:** image copyright David Rabkin 2010/used under license from www.shutterstock.com **99:** image copyright Dmitriy Shironosov/used under license from www.shutterstock.com **102:** image copyright jokerpro 2010/used under license from www.shutterstock.com **103:** Jupiterimages/Getty Images **104:** DNY59 /iStockphoto.com **105:** top left apomares/iStockphoto.com, top right VISUM Foto GmbH / Alamy, center left Michael Matthews - Police Images / Alamy, center right TommL/iStockphoto.com **109:** Michael Cogliantry/Photonica/Getty Images **110:** bottom center © Roger De La Harpe; Gallo Images/CORBIS, bottom right © ReligiousStock / Alamy **111:** all images copyright 2005 PhotoDisc Inc. **115:** James Tutor/iStockphoto.com **116:** bottom left image copyright Lowe Llaguno 2010/Used under license from Shutterstock.com, bottom center image copyright Monkey Business Images 2010/used under license from www.shutterstock.com, bottom right René Mansi/iStockphoto.com, top right image copyright Wayne Johnson 2010/used under license from www.shutterstock.com **117:** top left Dawn liljenquist/iStockphoto.com, center right image copyright Zuura 2010/used under license from www.shutterstock.com **121:** © Ron Niebrugge / Alamy **120:** image copyright Korionov 2010/used under license from www.shutterstock.com **124:** top oversnap/iStockphoto.com, bottom Warwick Lister-Kaye/iStockphoto.com **125:** center left image copyright worldswildlifewonders 2010/Used under license from Shutterstock.Com, center image copyright worldswildlifewonders 2010/Used under license from shutterstock.com, center kawisign/iStockphoto.com, center right image copyright Tamara Kulikova 2010/Used under license from shutterstock.com **126:** PAUL DAMIEN / National Geographic **127:** center right image copyright urosr 2009/Used under license from Shutterstock.com, bottom right BILL HATCHER/National geographic images **128:** top left image copyright A & S Aakjaer/used under license from www.shutterstock.com, top center image copyright juliengrondin 2010/Used under license from Shutterstock.Com, top center travis manley/iStockphoto.com, top right image copyright Kevin Gardner 2010/Used under license from Shutterstock.com **129:** right © JTB Photo Communications Inc. / Alamy, left© Reuters/CORBIS **130:** tl Jim West / Alamy, center image copyright EdBockStock 2009/Usesd under license from www.shutterstock .com, center Nathan Gleave/iStockphoto.com, top right Gino Santa Maria/iStockphoto.com, **132:** © Francesco Venturi/CORBIS **137:** Dmitriy Shironosov/iStockphoto.com

Scope & Sequence

Unit/Lesson	Vocabulary Link	Listening	Language Link
Unit 1: Indoors and Outdoors			
Lesson A At home p. 2 **Lesson B** Public spaces p. 7	* **Home improvement** p. 2 *rearrange, repairs, options* * **Public figures or private citizens?** p. 7 *privacy, rights, general public*	* **Colorful combinations** p. 3 Use background knowledge Make predictions from notes * **That's none of your business!** p. 8 Infer information Choose an appropriate response	* **Participles used as adjectives** p. 5 * **Expressing prohibition** p. 10
Unit 2: Life's Changes			
Lesson A The times of your life p. 12 **Lesson B** Milestones p. 17	* **Parent or friend?** p. 12 *grown-up, childhood, teenagers* * **A Cross-cultural ambassador** p. 17 *got married, went to school, left home*	* **A very special day** p. 13 Listen for context Guess the meaning of words * **Good times ahead** p. 18 Listen to infer information Listen for gist and detail	* **Review of future forms** p. 15 * **Modals of future possibility** p. 20
Unit 3: Getting Information			
Lesson A How we communicate p. 22 **Lesson B** In the news p. 27	* **We talk about everything.** p. 22 *gossip, chat, discuss, argue, share* * **Have you heard the news?** p. 27 *local news, word of mouth, in the news*	* **Ask all your friends!** p. 23 Inference Listen for details * **Your source for the news** p. 28 Listen for gist and detail	* **Participial and prepositional phrases** p. 25 * **Review of the present perfect** p. 30
Review Units 1–3 p. 32			
Unit 4: Men and Women			
Lesson A How do I look? p. 36 **Lesson B** Dating p. 41	* **I like to wear bright colors.** p. 36 wear *makeup,* get *a tattoo* * **A love story?** p. 41 *ask out, turn down, break up*	* **Say "cheese"!** p. 37 Use background knowledge Dictation * **I want to go out with him.** p. 42 Understand character relationships Listen for details	* **The present perfect with** *already, just, never, still,* **and** *yet* p. 39 * **Phrasal verbs** p. 44
Unit 5: Being Different			
Lesson A Mind your manners p. 46 **Lesson B** Adjusting to a new place p. 51	* **Good or bad behavior** p. 46 *appropriate, inconsiderate, polite* * **Cross-cultural communication** p. 51 *jet lag, body language, personal space*	* **Here are the rules.** p. 47 Listen for context Make predictions Listen to paraphrases * **We've been talking about . . .** p. 52 Listen for main topic Note-taking Make inferences	* *It + be* + **adjective + infinitive; gerund as subject** p. 49 * **Future time clauses** p. 54
Unit 6: Big Business			
Lesson A Success stories p. 56 **Lesson B** The ABCs of advertising p. 61	* **Talking about business** p. 56 *advertise, consume, purchase* * **Up and down** p. 61 *recover, in a slump, increase*	* **An article about email** p. 57 Choose the best answer * **Commercials** p. 62 Inference Listen for specific information	* **The passive: simple present and simple past** p. 59 * **Connecting words:** *because, so, although / even though* p. 64
Review Units 4–6 p. 66			

Pronunciation	Speaking & Speaking Strategy	Reading	Writing	Communication
Saying a series of items p. 3	**Why don't you fix it yourself?** p. 4 Making informal suggestions	**The father of American landscape architecture** p. 8 Make predictions from photos Find sentences to support your answers Find related words	**Classroom rules** p. 10 Make a list of dos and don'ts for the classroom	* **An improvement project** p. 6 Making improvements to a room * **Which place would you protect?** p. 11 Discussing the protection of natural and historical sites
Emphasis patterns p. 13	**I need a new license.** p. 14 Talking about plans and needs	**Life's stressors** p. 18 Use background knowledge Scan (timed)	**My future** p. 21 Write about possible events in the future	* **The Magic Answer Bag** p. 16 Playing a game of predicting the future * **What will you do?** p. 21 Taking a quiz about your future
Stress: verb + preposition p. 23	**Could I interrupt for a second?** p. 24 Interrupting someone politely	**Nutty news** p. 28 Use visual cues Scan for specific language or examples Sequence events	**An unusual news story** p. 31 Write a story about an unusual event	* **Your future job** p. 26 Interviewing a person to find their future job. * **Blogging** p. 31 Finding someone's future self
Different ways to say _ch_ p. 37	**I'm getting a tattoo!** p. 38 Disagreeing politely	**Ways to meet people** p. 42 Use background information Read for details Make inferences	**A personal ad** p. 45 Write a personal ad	* **Act like a man** p. 40 Discussing ideas about gender * **Dating Survey** p. 45 Taking and discussing the results of a dating survey
Linking the same sounds p. 47	**Mmm. It's delicious.** p. 48 Asking about customs	**JT's Travel Blog** p. 52 Scan for details Identify writer's tone Make predictions about what will happen next	**A language barrier** p. 55 Write about overcoming a language barrier	* **Subway rules** p. 50 Talking about what is polite and rude * **Help for the homesick** p. 55 Giving advice to homesick people
Stress on nouns and verbs with the same spelling p. 57	**People first!** p. 58 Emphasizing important points	**Is advertising necessary?** p. 62 Recognize opinions Scan for words	**Consumer advice** p. 65 Write a product review	* **What is made in your country?** p. 60 Creating a list of interesting facts about a place * **Rate the advertisement.** p. 65 Reviewing advertisements

Scope & Sequence

Unit/Lesson	Vocabulary Link	Listening	Language Link
Unit 7: Health			
Lesson A How do you feel? p. 70 **Lesson B Getting better** p. 75	* **Adventure on a mountain** p. 70 *drowsy, dizzy, shiver* * **I'm sick of it!** p. 75 *homesick, worried sick, call in sick*	* **A cold or the flu?** p. 71 Listen for specific information * **How's school?** p. 76 Listen for details Identify people	* **Verb + noun / adjective / verb(-ing); noun + hurt(s)** p. 73 * **Reported speech: requests and commands** p. 78
Unit 8: Sports and Hobbies			
Lesson A In my free time p. 80 **Lesson B The active life** p. 85	* **A great way to stay active** p. 80 *active member, where the action is, leisure time activity* * **Around the world by car** p. 85 *pay for, run on, know about*	* **It's time to renew it.** p. 81 Listen to Inference Listen for context * **Choose the best response.** p. 86 Listen to a statement and choose the best response	* **The present perfect vs. the present perfect continuous** p. 83 * **The simple past tense vs. the perfect tenses** p. 88
Unit 9: Social Issues			
Lesson A In my community p. 90 **Lesson B People, people, everywhere!** p.95	* **Are you old enough to vote?** p. 90 *make progress, vote for, taxes* * **The problem of sprawl** p. 95 *develop, development, force*	* **Together we can do it.** p. 91 Listen for speaker's attitude Listen for specific meaning Infer main points * **Urban or suburban?** p. 96 Use background information Inference	* *Too* and *enough* p. 93 * **Future real conditionals** p. 98
Review Units 7–9 p. 100			
Unit 10: Having It All			
Lesson A Money issues p. 104 **Lesson B Striking it rich** p. 109	* **Money quiz** p. 104 *get by, owe, short on money* * **You're a winner!** p. 109 *accept, claim, donate*	* **Rich and poor** p. 105 Listen for gist Inference * **Saving money, saving lives** p. 110 Listen for cause and effect Take notes	* *Wish*-**statements** p. 107 * **Negative modals** p. 112
Unit 11: Honestly Speaking			
Lesson A To tell the truth p. 114 **Lesson B Who do you trust?** p. 119	* **Tell me the truth.** p. 114 *against the law, depends on the circumstances, an exception* * **I have confidence in . . .** p. 119 *count on, trustworthy*	* **An empty desk** p. 115 Use background information Dictation * **I completely agree.** p. 120 Determine the correct response to a statement	* **Present unreal conditionals** p. 117 * **Reported statements** p. 122
Unit 12: Our Earth			
Lesson A The natural world p. 124 **Lesson B The man-made world** p. 129	* **Endangered animals** p. 124 *extinct, illegal, mascot* * **Great structures** p. 129 *construction, withstand, links*	* **Rainforest animals** p. 125 Listen for gist Define unfamiliar vocabulary * **An engineer's job** p. 130 Identify correct photos for listening Listen for details	* *Like* **as a preposition and a verb** p. 127 * **The passive with various tenses** p. 132
Review Units 10–12 p. 134			

1 Vocabulary Link Home improvement

A Look at the room below. Do you like it? Why or why not? What is one thing you would do to improve it?

 B Now read this article. Think of a room you know. Which tip is the most helpful? Discuss with a partner.

> rearrange = change position
> *verb object*
> rearrange furniture
>
> What do these *re-* verbs mean?
> retell   rewrite   reorganize
>
> What objects follow them?

TIPS ON WORKING
WITH A SMALL SPACE

No space? No money? No problem! When it comes to home improvement ideas, we turn to our home furnishings expert, Eudora West. Here are her simple tips:

COLOR
• Dark colors can make a small room look even smaller.
• Some colors, like orange and purple, can be overwhelming when used alone. Combine them with neutral colors, like beige and gray.

FURNITURE
• Large furniture doesn't work well in a small space.
• There are many space-saving options on the market. If you don't want to do anything new, you can rearrange the furniture you have.

MIRRORS
• One easy way to make a small space look bigger: use mirrors. Your room will immediately appear larger.

SIMPLE FIXES
• You can make a room look better quickly by fixing things that are broken. Can't do the repairs by yourself? Hire an expert to help you.

ASK ANSWER

Who repairs things in your home?
What works well in your bedroom right now?
What doesn't work well? How could you reorganize your room?

 C With a partner, choose one of the blue words or phrases in **B**. Look it up in your dictionary. Be prepared to explain it to the class.

2 Listening   **Colorful combinations**

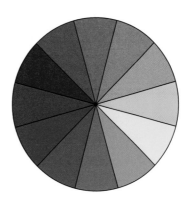

A Look at the picture of a color wheel. Answer these questions.

  1. When do you use a color wheel?

  2. Which colors do you think are warm? Which ones are cool?

CD 1
Track 2

B Read the chart and predict the answers. Then listen and complete the notes.

What the color wheel does	Shows us how to (1) _____ colors in an attractive way
People who use the color wheel	painters, decorators, and (2) _____ designers
Primary colors	red, (3) _____, and (4) _____
Use of these colors	can (5) _____ them together to create (6) _____
Warm colors	yellow and (7) _____
Their effect	They have a lot of (8) _____. They come (9) _____ the viewer.
Cool colors	blue and (10) _____
Their effect	They are quiet and (11) _____. They move (12) _____ from the viewer.

CD 1
Track 3

C Listen to the information about combining colors. Circle the correct picture.

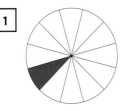   **1**   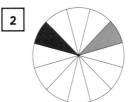   **2**      **3**

> **ASK   ANSWER**
>
> Look back at your answers in **B** and **C**. Explain the lecture in your own words.
>
> What is your favorite color combination? Why?

3 Pronunciation   **Saying a series of items**

CD 1
Track 4

A Listen to these sentences. Notice how the final item in a series has a falling intonation. Practice saying the sentences.

  1. The three primary colors on the color wheel are red, yellow, and blue.

  2. White, black, and gray are neutral colors.

  3. Our living room has a sofa, table, and two chairs.

  4. You can enlarge a space by using mirrors, light colors, and small furniture.

B Complete the chart below. Read and explain your answers to a partner.

My three favorite colors	
My hardest subjects in school	
My three favorite singers/actors	

> I really like red, white, and green. They're my favorites because...

4 Speaking   Why don't you fix it yourself?

A Emilia has just moved into a new apartment. Read the conversation and answer the questions.

CD 1
Track 5

- How does Emilia like the apartment? What's the problem?
- How does Felipe make suggestions to solve the problem? Underline the sentences.
- How does Emilia accept and refuse the advice? Circle the sentences.

Emilia: Thanks for your help, Felipe.

Felipe: No problem. How do you like your new apartment?

Emilia: It's great. I love it. There's just one thing . . .

Felipe: Yeah?

Emilia: I found a small crack in the wall.

Felipe: The wall is cracked? Really?

Emilia: Yeah. It's not too big, but it's in the living room and everyone can see it.

Felipe: Why don't you fix it yourself?

Emilia: Um . . . I don't think so. I'm not good at repairing things.

Felipe: I know! Try calling my friend, Sam. He can help you. He's a nice guy and he's very capable.

Emilia: That sounds like a great idea. Do you have his phone number?

Felipe: Sure. Hold on a second while I get it . . .

B Can you think of another way to solve Emilia's problem? What would you do? Tell your partner.

5 Speaking Strategy

Useful Expressions: Making informal suggestions	
With base form	**With verb + -ing**
Why don't you <u>fix</u> it yourself?	Have you thought about <u>fixing</u> it yourself?
I know what you should do. <u>Call</u> my friend.	Try <u>calling</u> my friend.

Read these two situations. Choose one and role play it.
Then switch roles and role play the other situation.

Student A: Tell your friend about your problem.
Practice accepting and refusing suggestions.
Student B: Use the expressions in the chart to make suggestions.

 Responding
Good idea!
That's a great idea.
Maybe I'll do that.
Sounds good to me.
I guess it's worth a try.
I don't think so.
No, I don't like that idea.

Problem: It's 2:00 a.m. You return home and can't find the key to your house. You're locked out! Your parents are sleeping and they will be angry if you wake them.

Problem: You have just moved into a new apartment. It has very few windows and is dark. You don't have a lot of money to spend on home decorating.

6 Language Link **Participles used as adjectives**

A Study the chart. Then complete the verb chart below. Look up any verbs you don't know.

Subject	Verb			Subject	Be	Past Participle
I	broke	the window.	⟶	The window	**is**	**broken.**
Water	froze	in the pipes.	⟶	The pipes	**are**	**frozen.**

• Past participle adjectives describe a state.

Present	Past	Past Participle	Present	Past	Past Participle
bend				cracked	
	burned		flood		
clog			jam		

B Use the verbs in **A** + *be* to describe the pictures below.

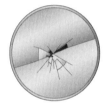

1. The mirror ___is cracked___.

2. The light bulbs
_____ out.

3. The basement
_____.

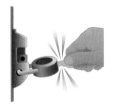

4. The lock _____.

5. The drain _____.

6. The keys _____.

C Complete the sentences with the correct form of the word in parentheses.

1. This room needs a lot of work. The walls _____ (crack) and the floor _____ (stain).

2. It rained a lot and now the house is _____ (flood).

3. Don't _____ (jam) the key into the lock. You don't want to _____ (break) it.

4. Someone _____ (break) the window last week. I can't believe it _____ still
_____ (break).

5. The little boy _____ (throw) something into the sink. Now the drain _____ (clog).

D Is there anything in your home that is broken or not working properly? How can you fix it? Tell a partner.

One of the cabinet doors is broken. It doesn't close properly.

Why don't you…

7 Communication An improvement project

 A Look at this picture of a local hospital waiting room. Answer the questions with a partner.

1. Would you like to visit this hospital? Why or why not?
2. What are some of the problems with this waiting room?
3. What can you do to fix some of these problems?

B Read about a contest.

- A local company wants to improve the room in **A**. They are sponsoring a design contest.
- You are going to enter the design contest. Using the picture in **A**, come up with at least five ideas for improving the room.
- Your goals are to make the room more welcoming and comfortable.
- The winning design team will receive $25,000!

 C Working with two partners, come up with some ideas for the design contest. Write them here.

OUR IDEAS TO MAKE THE ROOM MORE . . .	
welcoming	comfortable

 D Present your ideas. Take turns speaking and introducing yourself to the class.

Language for presentations	
Starting out	**Introducing yourself**
Hello, everyone. I'd like to thank you for coming. Let me tell you a little about myself.	My name is . . . I'm (name) from (school / company).

Indoors and Outdoors

Lesson B Public spaces

1 Vocabulary Link   Public figures or private citizens?

A Look at the photo on the right and read the information. Who are the paparazzi and what do they do? Why do they do it?

B Read the opinions below. Can you guess who said each one? Match a picture to each statement. Explain your choices to a partner.

> a. My private life is my own. What I do in my free time is none of your business.

> b. Singers and actors are public figures. The general public is interested in them. It's natural to have paparazzi following them. I work with the paparazzi all the time.

The paparazzi are photographers who follow famous people and take pictures of them. They then sell the photos to web sites and magazines.

> c. I'm a fan and I like to read about famous people. But I feel sorry for them. When they go out in public, the paparazzi follow them. Celebrities never have any privacy. That's hard.

> d. Movie stars, like all people, have certain rights. For example, you can't disturb (= bother) them in their own homes.

1. Clark, *Take a Look* magazine owner

2. Desiree, lawyer

3. Cesar, actor

4. Hong-li, student

Word Partnerships

These expressions go together with some form of the words *private* and *public*. Which one partners with only one of them?

~ life   ~ owned business

~ school ~ conversations

open to the ~

C Complete the chart below with blue words from **A**. Then tell a partner: How are the *public* and *private* phrases different?

Public	Private / Individual
1. a _____	1. a private citizen
2. the _____	2. one person
3. (do something) _____	3. (do something) in private
4. your public life	4. your _____

> A public figure is someone famous, like a movie star. But a private citizen...

D Which opinion(s) in **B** do you agree with? Why?

2 Listening   That's none of your business!

A You are going to listen to three conversations. Which statement (A, B, or C) is true about each conversation? Listen and circle the correct answer.

CD 1
Track 6

1. A. The two friends are fighting.
   B. The boy wants to talk to the girl.
   C. The girl is talking to her boyfriend.

2. A. Paula is studying.
   B. Paula has met Carla Smith.
   C. Carla Smith is a public figure.

3. A. The woman is a singer.
   B. They are talking in private.
   C. They are meeting for the first time.

B Read the sentences below. Then listen again. What might the person say next? Choose the best ending for each conversation. Two sentences are extra.

CD 1
Track 6

Conversation 1
Conversation 2
Conversation 3

a. She doesn't have any privacy. It's terrible!
b. They shouldn't speak to her in private like that. It's rude!
c. Sorry, but I don't talk about my private life on television.
d. Celebrities shouldn't do that in public.
e. Excuse me, but that's none of your business!

3 Reading   The father of American landscape architecture

A Look at the photos on page 9. Then choose the best definition to finish the sentence.

A landscape architect _____.

a. designs parks and gardens   b. builds schools   c. gives tours

Frederick Law Olmsted

B Read the article. Do you think these people would agree or disagree with these statements? Check (✓) your answers. Then find evidence that supports your answers.

1. **Jin Hee:** I'm always studying. I don't have time to appreciate the campus.
   ☐ agree   ☐ disagree _____ *lines 4-5*

2. **Alejandro Vega:** Central Park is large, but it has a cozy feeling.
   ☐ agree   ☐ disagree _____

3. **Ross Howard:** Niagara Falls is totally open to the public.
   ☐ agree   ☐ disagree _____

4. **Olmsted:** I don't participate in design contests. They're silly.
   ☐ agree   ☐ disagree _____

5. **Olmsted:** We should keep the natural feeling of these places.
   ☐ agree   ☐ disagree _____

6. **Olmsted:** I care about the animals in the state park.
   ☐ agree   ☐ disagree _____

C Find words in the reading that are related in form to the ones below. What part of speech is each word? Use your dictionary for help. Check your answers with a partner.

1. beauty   _beautiful (adjective)_
2. access   _____
3. produce _____

4. nature   _____
5. development _____
6. litter   _____

Creating Public Spaces

Jin Hee Park is a student at Stanford University in California. She studies hard. "Of course, I came here for the academics," she says. "But it doesn't hurt that the campus is so beautiful. I walk around sometimes just to
5 relax."

Alejandro Vega, a banker in New York City, jogs almost every evening after work in Central Park. "I never get bored. The park is so big. It's a public space, yet it can feel completely private."

10 Niagara Falls was on Ross Howard's list of places to visit in upstate New York. "There are these wonderful footpaths that make the falls so accessible to the general public. You can get really close."

In 1857, a design contest was held for a new park in New
15 York City. Frederick Law Olmsted and his partner, Calvert Vaux, won the contest. Central Park was the finished product—the first landscaped public park in the United States. Today, no trip to New York is complete without a visit to this beautiful park.

20 Later in his life, Olmsted designed landscapes for college campuses, including Stanford University. He also designed footpaths at Niagara Falls to give visitors better views of the falls. In all his work, Olmsted tried to preserve* the natural beauty of an area.

Central Park

Niagara Falls

25 Today there are new pressures on Niagara Falls: some businesses want to develop the area. On Goat Island, an island in Niagara Falls State Park, there are now souvenir shops. There may be signs that
30 say "No Littering," but there is still a lot of trash on the island. Most of the animals have disappeared. What would Olmsted think?

*preserve = save and protect

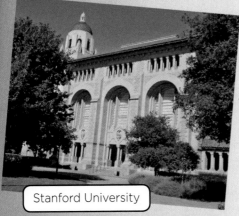
Stanford University

ASK ANSWER

What's your favorite park?
How can public parks be preserved?

4 Language Link — Expressing prohibition

A Study the chart. Complete the missing sentences in the chart by matching the information below. Where do you think you would hear these sentences?

Expressing Prohibition

be allowed to / *c* **be supposed to**	**1.** Sir, you aren't allowed to <u>park</u> your car here today. ___*on the street (from a police officer)*___ **2.** Remember, you aren't supposed to <u>touch</u> the paintings. _____
with modals	**3.** I'm sorry, but you can't <u>use</u> your cell phone inside. _____ **4.** You mustn't <u>drink and drive</u> at the same time. _____
with –ing forms	**5.** Actually, there's no <u>smoking</u> on the platform. _____ **6.** <u>Talking</u> is not permitted during the exam. _____

a. Once you receive your paper, you may begin.

b. Please step out onto the balcony.

c. Please use the parking lot.

d. Please wait until you exit the station.

e. They're very old.

f. You could have a serious accident.

B Work with a partner. Make a short conversation. Use at least two expressions in **A**. Perform your conversation for the class.

A: I'm sorry, but you can't park here today.

B: But why not, officer? I always park here on Saturdays.

A: Well, today is different. They're shooting a movie. There's no parking allowed all day today.

B: Oh, OK. What should I do then?

A: There's a parking garage near here.

B: How do I get there?

A: Well, go two blocks and . . .

C Think of two rules for each of the places below. Tell your partner.

> airplane   swimming pool   movie theater

> You're not supposed to use your cell phone during the flight. You have to wait until the plane lands.

5 Writing — Classroom rules

A With a partner, make a list of five rules for your classroom.

> 1. You can't leave class early.
> 2. You aren't allowed to chew gum in school.

B Now imagine your dream classroom. Rewrite the rules in **A**.

> 1. You can leave class 10 minutes early if you're bored.
> 2. You're allowed to chew gum anytime in school.

C Join another pair. Compare your lists. Then read them to the class.

> Which country was the first to ban smoking in all work places?
> a. The United States   b. The Republic of Ireland   c. Sweden

6 Communication   **Which place would you protect?**

A   Read about these five places. Which one is the most interesting to you?

The Galapagos Islands (Ecuador)
Unique island "natural museum"

1,000 km from South America, these 19 islands have animals and plants that developed without humans around.
Problem: Taking animals from the islands isn't permitted, but humans have still damaged the islands by introducing unfamiliar plants and animals.

Venice and its lagoon (Italy)
Famous cultural city

Founded in the 5th century, romantic Venice lies on 18 islands and people travel by boats.
Problem: The water is rising every year and causing even more damage.

Angkor (Cambodia)
Magnificent ancient city

It contains ruins of more than 100 temples from the 9th to 15th centuries. It covers 400 sq. km.
Problem: People aren't allowed to visit some parts of the city because the areas are falling apart and are unsafe.

Timbuktu (Mali)
Ancient spiritual capital

It was a center for Islam in the 15th and 16th centuries. There are old buildings, including famous mosques.
Problem: Desert sands are covering up the city.

Lake Baikal (Russia)
World's oldest and deepest lake

It contains 20% of the world's unfrozen freshwater and an unusual variety of marine and plant life.
Problem: You're not supposed to pollute the lake, but people still do it.

B   Imagine that you are on a special committee for the United Nations. You must choose one place to protect for the future. Consider the questions below to help you with your decision. Report your decision to the class.

Is the place important to history?	Is it beautiful?
Is it rare or unique?	Does it teach us about the earth?
Is it very old?	Are the problems easy to fix?
Will many people visit it?	Is it disappearing quickly?

   Check out the World Link video.

   Practice your English online at http://elt.heinle.com/worldlink

2 Life's Changes

Lesson A   The times of your life

1 Vocabulary Link   Parent or friend?

A   How would you describe your relationship with your parents? Check (✓) the box.
Explain your answer to a partner.

❑ We're all busy. We don't see each other that much.

❑ I think my parents are too strict. They should relax a little.

❑ We're like best friends. We talk about everything.

❑ other (your idea): _____

B   Read the article. What is it about?

- In a survey of 1,000 parents and 500 children, 43% of the grown-ups said they wanted to be their children's "best friend."

- 40% said they wanted to buy their children everything they wanted.

Peggy, a parent with a young son, said "My childhood was difficult. We didn't have any money. I want to give my son everything he asks for."

Fred, a single dad, says "Adulthood is all about responsibility. Adolescence* is all about having fun. I don't want my children to work too hard."

Dr. Julio Garcia, a childcare specialist, says that "Children need an adult to rely on. They need rules—and a best friend isn't going to give you rules."

Interestingly, the youth in the survey didn't share their parents' values.

- When they are ready to start a family, only 28% of teens and young adults want to be their children's best friends.

- Only 10% want to buy their kids everything.

*adolescence = teenage years

 Use *the* + adjective to talk about groups of people in general. Can you add some examples?

the elderly / the y_____

the rich / the p_____

the unemployed / the e_____

C   Which blue words in **B** describe grown-ups and what they do?
Which ones describe children and teenagers? Write the words
in the box. Which words are more informal than others?

Grown Ups	Children and teenagers

ASK ANSWER

Look again at the article in **B**. Whose opinion (the adults' or the teens') do you agree with? Why?
At what age does a teenager become a young adult?
What do people do to celebrate or mark this event?

2 Listening **A very special day**

A Have you ever given or listened to a speech? What was it about?

B You are going to hear a speech. Listen and answer the questions below.

1. This speech is being given at a(n) _____.

    a. wedding   c. birthday celebration

    b. office party   d. graduation ceremony

2. What information in the speech helped you choose your answer? Write the key words below.

   key words: _____

C Listen again to parts of the speech. What does the speaker mean when she says these things?

1. "You are joining the work world with all its responsibilities. In short, you are leaving your comfort zone."

    a. You will face many unfamiliar situations.

    b. Your life will become more comfortable.

    c. It's not so difficult to find a job.

2. "No matter what, though, you were always driven to succeed. And now you are here today. Congratulations."

    a. Your classes were difficult and required a lot of thinking.

    b. You never gave up and you should feel proud.

    c. You worried about today and not being successful.

3. "Shoot for the moon. Even if you miss it, you will land among the stars."

    a. Make a plan and ask for help.

    b. Travel a lot and experience new things.

    c. Try your hardest at everything you do.

> **ASK ANSWER**
>
> Think about the last speech you heard. Where were you? What was the speaker saying?

3 Pronunciation **Emphasis patterns**

A Listen to the following sentences. Notice how the <u>underlined</u> content words (nouns, verbs, adjectives, and adverbs) are stressed.

1. She's <u>spending</u> the <u>weekend</u> in the <u>city</u>.

2. Our <u>class</u> <u>begins</u> on <u>Monday</u>.

3. I'm going to <u>work</u> <u>hard</u> and <u>save</u> my <u>money</u>.

4. As a <u>young</u> <u>adult</u>, I have more <u>responsibilities</u>.

5. I <u>come</u> from a <u>big</u> <u>family</u>. My <u>childhood</u> was <u>really</u> <u>fun</u>.

B With a partner, take turns reading the sentences in **A**. Be sure to stress the content words.

4 Speaking   **I need a new license.**

CD 1
Track 10

A Read the conversation between Yuri and Max.
Then read the three false statements about Max.
Correct them and make them true.

1. Max doesn't know how to drive.

2. His driver's license disappeared.

3. He's traveling in two days.

Yuri: What are you studying for, Max?

Max: Oh, hi, Yuri . . . just my driving test.

Yuri: Your driving exam? Don't you have a driver's
license already?

Max: I had one . . . but it expired*, so I have to take
the test again.

Yuri: That's a drag.

Max: Yeah, and I need to get my license soon.

Yuri: How come?

Max: I'm planning to visit my cousins in two weeks. I need to rent a
car for the trip.

Yuri: Sounds like fun. Well, good luck with everything!

* expire = to come to an end

B Practice the conversation with a partner.

Useful Expressions
Talking about plans
I'm planning to rent a car.
I'm going to visit my cousins.
I'm thinking about taking a trip.
Talking about needs
I need (to get) a driver's license.

5 Speaking Strategy

A What do you think are these people's plans or intentions?
What do they need to do? Share your ideas with a partner. Use the expressions
in the Useful Expressions box.

Penny

Diego

Tisha

B Check (✓) the items you plan to do in the future. Add one more item to the list.

- ☐ take a big trip
- ☐ vote in an election
- ☐ apply for a credit card
- ☐ move
- ☐ buy _____
- ☐ _____

C Tell your partner what you plan to do and when. What do you need to do to make it happen?

6 Language Link   Review of future forms

A   Study the chart. Then match the questions to their answers. Which sentences describe a prediction, a plan, etc.?

	Will	Be going to
Make a prediction	The economy will improve.	The economy is going to improve.
State a plan	— — — — — — — — — — — — — —	I'm going to visit Brazil in May.
Something about to happen	— — — — — — — — — — — — — —	Uh-oh . . . I'm going to sneeze!
	Present continuous	**Simple present**
Scheduled events	The store opens at 10:00.	The store is opening at 10:00.

1. Do you think he'll have a happy childhood?
2. What are you doing for summer vacation?
3. How will life be different in the future?
4. What time is your graduation?
5. Is Tina pregnant?

a. We're going to have robots doing a lot of the work for us.
b. Yes, she's going to have her baby any day now.
c. Absolutely. He has two wonderful, loving parents.
d. The ceremony begins at noon.
e. We're not going to do anything special. I just want to relax!

B   Complete the conversation below. Use a future form of the verbs in parentheses. In some cases, there may be more than one answer possible.

A: I (1. fly) _____ to Thailand tomorrow.
   My plane (2. leave) _____ at 4:00.

B: Oh, really?

A: Yes. I (3. visit) _____ my friend in Bangkok.

   There's only one problem. I don't have a ride to the airport.

B: Don't worry. I have a car. I (4. take) _____ you.

A: Thanks. Do you think I (5. need) _____ these sweaters?

B: No. It (6. be) _____ warm there.

C   Complete the sentences below with a list of your personal plans and predictions. Then share your answers with a partner.

Plans

   Tonight, I _____

   This weekend, I _____

Predictions

   Ten years from now, I think _____

   Fifty years from now, I think _____

> I'm going to see a movie tonight with my friends. It starts at 7:00.

> What are you going to see?

7 Communication   **The Magic Answer Bag**

> The Magic Answer Bag can tell your fortune. You ask it a question and then reach in and pull out your answer.

A   In groups of 3 or 4, write each expression from the box below on a slip of paper and fold each paper. Each group puts their papers in a bag or hat.

Yes	No	Maybe
Absolutely!	No way!	It's possible.
For sure!	Not a chance!	Maybe.
Of course!	It's not going to happen!	Who knows?

B   What would you like to know about your future?
Think of four *yes/no* questions and write them down. Do not show anyone yet.

Example: Will I get a good grade on my next exam?

1. _____
   _____

2. _____
   _____

3. _____
   _____

4. _____
   _____

C   You are now going to get answers to your questions. Ask the Magic Answer Bag your question. A member of your group should shake the bag, pull out an answer, and read it aloud.

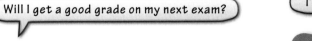
Will I get a good grade on my next exam?

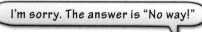
I'm sorry. The answer is "No way!"

D   Discuss the Magic Answer Bag's answers.
Do you think they were accurate? Why or why not?

> **ASK ANSWER**
> Do you think some people or things can predict the future? Explain your answer.

Life's Changes

Lesson B   Milestones

1   Vocabulary Link   A Cross-cultural ambassador

A   Match the words in column A with those in B. Then read the story about Fran Turner. Use the expressions to complete the story. (Remember to use the past tense if necessary!)

A	B
be get have	born married children divorced

At first, Fran Turner's life wasn't so different. Like many women, she fell in love and (1) _____. Fran got pregnant and the couple (2) _____ two _____. She and her husband bought a house. Fran got a job as a lawyer's assistant while she also raised her family. Fran proudly watched her daughters grow up. She was your typical "working mom."

Over the years, however, things changed. One of Fran's daughters graduated from high school. Another left home and enrolled in college. Fran went to school at the University of Vermont and studied journalism. Fran and her husband also began to grow apart. She never really expected to (3) _____—but her marriage was over.

Fran (4) _____ in 1952. And in 1998, at the age of 46, she decided to take a trip to Central America—to think about things. Fran realized she liked traveling. For the last 15 years, she has traveled around the world, meeting new people, learning about new cultures, and writing about her experiences for travel magazines. She lives the life of a "cross-cultural ambassador." And Fran is probably not going to retire anytime soon!

Fran Turner

> **How are these expressions the same or different?**
>
> They're getting married.   They got married.
>
> They're planning to get married.   They're married.
>
> She's marrying him.

B   Look again at the expressions in blue in **A**. When do these events typically happen in one's life: childhood, adolescence, or adulthood? Complete the rest of the box with present tense forms.

childhood	was born,
adolescence	
adulthood	

C   Don't look at **A**. Use the expressions in **B** to retell Fran's story to a partner. Use the past tense.

2 Listening   Good times ahead

A Look at the blue vocabulary words on page 17. Which of life's events are you looking forward to? Which ones do you want to avoid?

CD 1
Track 11

B Lindsay is reading a magazine article. Listen and choose the best title for the article.

a. Is your life happy?

b. How can you get the best job?

c. Which life event is the happiest?

d. Are you a happy teen?

CD 1
Track 12

C Listen. Check (✓) the life event each person chooses. Take notes of key words that explain the reasons for the person's answer.

Person	Event		Reasons
Mark	❑ getting a job	❑ leaving home	
Lindsay	❑ getting married	❑ having children	
Dad	❑ getting a promotion	❑ retiring	

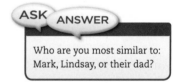

ASK ANSWER

Who are you most similar to: Mark, Lindsay, or their dad?

3 Reading   Life's stressors

What comes to mind when you hear the word *stress*?

Make a note of any words or images. Share your ideas with a partner.

A In each pair below, which event do you think causes more stress? Check (✓) the boxes. Explain your answer to a partner.

1. a. ❑ death of a spouse   2. a. ❑ pregnancy   3. a. ❑ divorce

   b. ❑ personal injury   b. ❑ retirement   b. ❑ moving

B Read the first part of the article about life's stressors on page 19 and compare the information in the article with your answers in **A**.

C Circle the correct answer.

Dr. Palmer thinks stressors are _____ events.

a. comfortable and uncomfortable

b. avoidable and unavoidable

c. major and minor

COPING WITH LIFE'S STRESSORS

by Dr. Judy Palmer

Let's face it: Life is stressful. Stressful events in our lives are called "stressors." Some of them are minor, such as uncomfortable air conditioning or a loudly ringing telephone. Others are more serious, such as the death of a spouse. That event tops the list as life's most stressful event.

You might be surprised to learn about the top 20 life stressors. Getting a divorce, for example, is number 2 on the list. And not all stressors are unhappy events. Pregnancy is a happy time for most families. It may also cause stress. Pregnancy is right below retirement on the list of life's major stressors.

We can't avoid stress, but we can do something about it. Read below to learn about the healthy responses these people had to stress in their lives.

Tina Vega, 16
Last year was horrible! My family moved to another town. I had to change schools and say good-bye to all my friends. It was really tough. I felt so lonely in my new school. But then one day I decided to enjoy my life: I smiled at everyone and I joined the soccer club at school. Now I have new friends. I like my new school.

Frederick Cho, 42
Life is unpredictable. Three weeks ago I lost my job. I was upset for the first week. I couldn't do anything. Now I'm looking for a new job. It's not good to sit around the house. I exercise every day and I'm healthier than I've been in years.

Hazel Greene, 80
My husband and I got married in 1960. He died five years ago. For the first two years I was depressed. I missed him so much because we did everything together. But now I'm feeling better. I think it's important to stay active and positive. I read a lot and do volunteer work.

D Scan the article and complete the chart below. You have two minutes.

	What happened?	When did it happen?	How did the person feel at first?	What did the person do to relieve stress?
Tina Vega	She moved to a new town.			
Frederick Cho		three weeks ago		
Hazel Greene			depressed	

ASK ANSWER

Do you think life nowadays is more or less stressful than it was 50 years ago? Why?

4 Language Link   Modals of future possibility

A   Study the chart. Notice the modals of future possibility highlighted in blue.

Modals of future possibility	
Questions	**Answers**
Are you going to go to college?	I may (not).
Will you go to college?	I might (not).
	I could.
When are you getting married?	I may/might/could get married next summer.

The blue modal verbs in the chart indicate that something is possible in the future. They are all very similar in meaning when used this way.

B   What will you do tomorrow? Check (✓) the box for *yes* (Y), *no* (N), or *maybe* (M). Ask your partner about his or her answers.

Y N M
1. get to class / work on time   ☐ ☐ ☐
2. do English homework   ☐ ☐ ☐
3. talk on the telephone a lot   ☐ ☐ ☐
4. watch a lot of TV   ☐ ☐ ☐
5. eat lunch alone   ☐ ☐ ☐
6. bring an umbrella   ☐ ☐ ☐

> Do you think you'll watch a lot of TV?

> I might not. There's nothing good on TV these days.

C   Read the sentences. How possible are these situations in the next year? five years? in your lifetime? Complete each one with *will/won't* or *may (not)*, *might (not)*, and *could*. Add two ideas of your own.

1. Scientists _____ be able to solve the global warming problem.
2. World hunger _____ end.
3. We _____ travel to other planets.
4. The world's population _____ decrease (go down).
5. _____
6. _____

D   Explain your answers to a partner.

> I'm afraid scientists may not be able to solve the global warming problem in my lifetime.

> I don't know...Maybe they could do it. We can't give up yet!

WORLD LINK

What year is the Earth's population expected to hit 9 billion?
a. year 2040
b. year 2050
c. year 2060

5 Writing — My future

A Look at the timeline. Then make a future timeline of your life. Put at least four events on it.

B Write about the events on your timeline that *will* happen and the ones that *may* happen. Give details.

C Share your writing with a partner. Ask and answer questions about the events on your timelines.

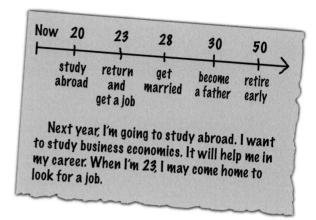

Now 20 23 28 30 50

study abroad | return and get a job | get married | become a father | retire early

Next year, I'm going to study abroad. I want to study business economics. It will help me in my career. When I'm 23, I may come home to look for a job.

6 Communication — What will you do?

A Complete this quiz about your future life.

have at least two children

get a big job promotion

	I may/might	I will	I won't
1. have at least two children			
2. get married more than once			
3. retire in 30 years			
4. graduate early			
5. get a big job promotion			
6. live alone			
7. travel somewhere fun or exciting			
8. see or meet a famous person			
9. find a job using English			
10. get a driver's license			
11. leave home before age 20			
12. buy a home			

B Interview your partner. Ask and answer questions about the chart above.

Do you think you'll have at least two children?

I might. I like kids a lot!

I know I won't. It's challenging to raise a large family.

C Join another pair. Explain how you are similar to or different from each other.

 Check out the World Link video.   Practice your English online at http://elt.heinle.com/worldlink

1 Vocabulary Link   We talk about everything.

A   Read what these people say. Notice the words in blue. Which ones can have a negative meaning?

I gossip with friends in a cafe. We chat about everything from celebrities to who's dating whom. We share our deepest secrets.

Some people don't know how to talk to others easily because they're shy. I wrote a book called "How to strike up a conversation with anyone."

I send a lot of text messages to my friends. One day last week I sent over 50 messages. It's easier and quicker than calling someone.

When we were kids, we argued all the time. We don't fight anymore—in fact, now we're really close. We discuss everything and ask each other for advice.

B   Talk about your own experiences with a partner. Use the blue words in **A**.

A: When I was a kid, I argued with my sister a lot, too.
B: Really? Not me. I didn't argue with my little brother at all.

C   Complete the sentences with the <u>noun form</u> of the words in the chart. In some cases, more than one word is possible. Use your dictionary for help.

verbs	nouns
argue	argument
chat	chat
converse	conversation
discuss	discussion
talk	talk

1. We had a long _____ about the situation at work.

2. They got into a big _____ and started shouting.

3. She's giving a _____ on the new proposal later today.

4. It's impossible to carry on a _____ here. It's too noisy.

5. I hadn't seen her in a long time. We had a very nice _____.

D   Ask and answer these questions with a partner.

1. What does your family typically chat about over dinner?

2. What's a topic you could confidently give a talk on?

3. What are some things you can do to avoid getting into an argument with someone?

4. What's the hardest thing about carrying on a conversation in English?

5. When did you last have a discussion with your teacher? What did you talk about?

2 Listening · Ask all your friends!

A Look at the names of the online sites below.
Which ones do you know?
Which site(s) do you use?

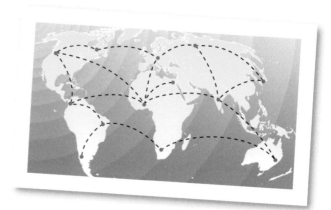

Facebook	MySpace	Orkut
Renren	LinkedIn	Mixi	hi5

your idea: _____

CD 1
Track 13

B Read the questions below. Then listen to an advertisement for a new online service.
Which question might you ask with the service?

a. Do you own a cell phone?

b. Can I borrow your cell phone?

c. What's an affordable cell phone?

d. What's the best thing about cell phones?

CD 1
Track 13

C Listen again. Complete the summary about InstaHelp and how it works.

When you have a question, it's easy to waste time looking for

(1) _____ online. InstaHelp is an (2) _____

service. You ask an important (3) _____ by

(4) _____ or instant message. InstaHelp

(5) _____ it on to some of your online

(6) _____ (and their acquaintances too).

You then get live answers back in (7) _____

minutes or so.

> **ASK · ANSWER**
>
> Look back at your answers in Exercise **C** and explain to a partner how the InstaHelp service works. Would you use it? Why or why not?

3 Pronunciation · Stress: verb + preposition

CD 1
Track 14

A Look at the two underlined words in each question. Which one is stressed? Listen and check your answers.

1. Who do you <u>talk</u> <u>to</u> when you have a problem?

2. What do you <u>talk</u> <u>about</u> with your friends?

3. What is everyone <u>gossiping</u> <u>about</u> these days?

4. Do you need to <u>discuss</u> anything <u>with</u> your teacher?

5. Who do you <u>chat</u> <u>with</u> the most on the phone?

B Practice saying the sentences. Ask and answer the questions with a partner.

4 Speaking   **Could I interrupt for a second?**

CD 1
Track 15

A   Read the conversation. Answer the questions.
1. What does Jared need?
2. What is Ana's advice?
3. Does Jared know Ms. Ruiz? How do you know?

Ana: Oh, look . . . there's Gloria Ruiz. Do you know her?

Jared: No, I don't. Who is she?

Ana: She's the VP of Marketing for Global Industries. She's standing right over there.

Jared: Is she the tall woman in the sweater?

Ana: No, Gloria is the woman with glasses. She's chatting with the man in the suit.

Jared: You know, I *am* looking for a job.

Ana: You should talk to her. Maybe she can help you.

Jared: That's a good idea. Thanks!

....

Jared: Excuse me, Ms. Ruiz? May I interrupt for a moment? My name is Jared Levy . . .

B   Practice the conversation with a partner.

5 Speaking Strategy

A   Think of a time you interrupted someone. Who were you talking to? What were you talking about?

> My friend and I were talking about our homework. I interrupted her because the bus was coming!

B   Role play. Work in groups of three. Use the language from the Useful Expressions box to help you.

Student 1: You are at a party. You need to interrupt two people who are having a conversation. Choose a reason below.

- You think you know Student 2. You want to introduce yourself.
- You need directions from the party to another place.
- Your idea: _____
  _____
  _____

Students 2 and 3: You are chatting. Student 1 will interrupt your conversation. Ask him or her at least two questions.

Useful Expressions: Interrupting someone politely
Introducing yourself
Excuse me. May I interrupt for a moment? My name is . . . I'm sorry to interrupt. / I beg your pardon. I just wanted to introduce myself. My name is . . .
Interrupting someone you know
Excuse me. Sorry to bother you, (name), but I have a question. Could I interrupt for a second? I just wanted to say/ask something.

6 Language Link   Participial and prepositional phrases

A Read the question and answers in the chart. Notice the different phrases used to describe people.

	Participial (*-ing*) phrases	Prepositional phrases
Do you know Joe Smith?	**He's the guy** chatting on the phone.	**He's the guy** on the phone.
	He's the person wearing a suit.	**He's the man** in a suit.
	He's the one standing near the door.	**He's the guy** with (the) black hair.

B Write questions about the people in the picture. (Use the words in parentheses.)
Start your questions with "Do you know . . . ?"

Do you know . . .

1. (talk / bus driver) _____ *Do you know the woman talking to the bus driver?* _____

2. (listen / music) _____

3. (skateboard and backpack) _____

4. (school uniforms) _____

5. (talk / phone) _____

C Choose a person in the picture. Don't tell your partner. Your partner guesses the person.

Is it someone with a briefcase?

Yes, it is.

Is it the woman talking to the bus driver?

No, it's not. Keep guessing.

7 Communication   **Your future job**

A Look at these jobs. What are they? Make a list. Add other jobs to your list.

B You are going to interview a partner and then suggest a job for him or her. First write some interview questions. Use the key words to get started.

1. work in one place / travel a lot
   Do you like/prefer to work in one place or travel a lot?

2. work and make decisions alone / discuss issues with others *Are you better at working and making decisions*
   alone or discussing issues with others?

3. be happy / be well paid

4. a quiet, predictable schedule / a busy, unpredictable schedule

5. chat in English / write in English

6. work indoors / work outdoors

7. strike up a conversation with a stranger / give a presentation to a small group

8. your question: _____

> **Do you like to work in one place or travel a lot?**

> **I like to travel, but not for work...so my answer is "work in one place." How about you?**

C Based on your partner's answers, choose a future job for him or her. How does your partner like your suggestion?

A: Let's see . . . you like to travel a lot and you like a busy, unpredictable schedule, right?

B: Yes, that's correct.

A: Plus, you're good at chatting in English.

B: Well, I know basic conversational English.

A: That's great! I think you should be a flight attendant for an international airline. You can travel and practice your English at the same time!

Getting Information

Lesson B In the news

1 Vocabulary Link   Have you heard the news?

A   Look at these three kinds of news programs. What are the names of some
popular news shows where you live? Why are those particular shows popular?

B   Take this quiz.

> **1.** How do you typically get your news?
> _____
>
> **2.** I am most interested in . . .
> ❏ international (world) news   ❏ local news (about my town or city)
> ❏ national news (about my country)
> because _____
>
> **3.** Which of these TV programs do you watch and how often do you watch them?
> ❏ cable news channels   ❏ morning news programs
> ❏ nightly network news   ❏ entertainment news
>
> **4.** When you learn a juicy piece of news, who do you tell first? _____
>
> **5.** Think of someone famous who was recently in the news.
> Who was it? _____
> Why was the person discussed so much in the media? (newspapers, magazines, radio,
> and TV)? _____
>
> **6.** Think again about the news story in #5. How did you hear the news?
> ❏ on TV   ❏ on the radio   ❏ in the newspaper   ❏ online
> ❏ by word of mouth. (= Someone told me.)
> Did you tell anyone else the news? If so, how many people did you tell? _____
>
> **7.** Which do you think is a better news source: traditional media (newspapers,
> magazines, radio, TV, etc.) or new media (Internet sources). Why? _____
> _____
> _____

   C   Explain your quiz answers to a partner.

> Usually from TV, I guess. I never read newspapers.

> How do you typically get your news?

2 Listening   Your source for the news

A What do these words mean? Can you write their opposites?

1. reliable → _____   2. _____ → inaccurate

Which news source do you think is most reliable? most inaccurate?

CD 1
Track 16

B Listen to the reporter and complete the sentence below.

The news report is about _____ from many countries _____.

a. young adults; and how often they watch the news   c. young adults; and where they get their news

b. young adults; who are in the news   d. older adults; and where they get their news

CD 1
Track 17

C Study the charts and listen to the entire report. Complete the charts with the correct letter.

A online

B cable news

C newspaper

Main Source for News

radio
5%

15%

40%

Entertainment
news
20%

20%

News knowledge

75%
60%
45%
30%
15%
0%

A international news

B national news

C local news

3 Reading   Nutty news

> **ASK ANSWER**
>
> Which do the people from the survey trust more: traditional or new media? Why? Which do you trust more?

A Look at the two photos on page 29. Then use the words below to make a title for each news article.

hero   office   hopping   wet

B You have one minute. Scan the articles and underline examples of the present perfect. (The first one has been done for you.)

C Read the first article. Number the events in the order they happened. (One statement is extra.) Then retell the story to a partner using the appropriate verb forms.

a. ___ Lulu barks like a dog.   d. ___ The family finds Ken.   g. ___ Lulu's mother dies.

b. ___ Lulu is adopted.   e. ___ Lulu leaves the zoo.   h. ___ Ken has an accident.

c. ___ Ken is unconscious.   f. ___ Lulu goes everywhere with Ken.

D Read the second article. What do these pairs of items have in common? Write your answers and then compare them with a partner's.

1. visit waterfalls / take an aerial tour _____ *These are things you can do in Vanuatu.* _____

2. scuba diving / snorkeling _____

3. three meters below the surface / near Port Vila _____

4. buy waterproof postcards / receive a special stamp _____

① *Local news* *.com

Our _____ _____

Lulu is a kangaroo. For 10 years she <u>has lived</u> with the Richards family. Lulu was adopted by the family after they found her next to her dead mother.

Mr. Ken Richards is a farmer. He was working on his farm when a heavy tree branch suddenly fell on top of him. It knocked him unconscious.

Lulu stood next to Mr. Richards' body. She started barking and didn't leave Mr. Richards' side.

"I've never heard Lulu bark like that—she sounded like a dog. She barked and barked and she didn't stop," said Celeste, Mr. Richards' daughter.

After 15 minutes, the Richards family went to investigate. They found Ken on the ground.

"Lulu is a hero," said Celeste. "She saved my father."

Mr. Middleton, an expert veterinarian, said that Lulu's story is rare. "I have never seen a kangaroo act like that. Maybe Lulu helped Ken Richards because the Richards family is the only family she has ever known."

Lulu is a loyal, friendly, and very intelligent kangaroo. After Ken leaves the hospital, he is planning to go everywhere with Lulu.

② *International news* *.com

This post _____ is all _____ !

The Republic of Vanuatu has recently been in the news —but not for the usual reasons!

Approximately 175,000 people live in the Republic of Vanuatu, an island chain east of Australia. It is a popular tourist destination because there's a lot to do there: you can visit waterfalls, go horseback riding, take an aerial tour, or visit a traditional Ni-Vanuatu village. Vanuatu is most famous for its scuba diving and snorkeling.

In an effort to draw attention to these popular water sports, Vanuatu has created a world's "first": the government has opened an underwater post office. You have to be a certified scuba diver to work there. The office is three meters below the surface in an area on the outskirts of Port Vila, the capital city.

So far, the post office has hired four workers. They will work in a room surrounded by the beauty of Vanuatu's underwater world. Customers will buy waterproof postcards on land and then dive down to the post office to receive a special waterproof stamp.

The word waterproof is in the second article. What does it mean? What do these other words ending in *-proof* mean?

fireproof   bulletproof

Do you know any others?

4 Language Link   Review of the present perfect

 Be careful!

For events at a specific time (period) in the past, use the simple past.

I lived in Tokyo from 2008-2009.

I bought that magazine yesterday.

A   Study the chart. Then complete the news story below with the verbs in parentheses. Use the present perfect or the simple past.

Using the Present Perfect

Use the present perfect for actions that began in the past and continue in the present.

I've worked for the same network news program for ten years.

You can also use the present perfect to talk about actions that happened in the past, when the time they happened isn't important.

Have you ever seen this program?

Use the present perfect with *just* for an action that has been completed recently.

I've just told them the news. Everyone's surprised!

Bruno Hoffman lives near Toft Park. Every morning for the past 10 years, he (1. take) _____ a walk in the park.

Yesterday a strange thing (2. happen) _____. In the park, a squirrel (3. jump) _____ onto his shoulder. It wouldn't leave. When Bruno (4. brush) _____ it off, it (5. jump) _____ up again.

At that point, Bruno (6. call) _____ the police. "A friendly squirrel (7. attack) _____ just _____ me," he said.

"I (8. hear) _____ never _____ of such a thing," said the police officer. He (9. advise) _____ Bruno to call an animal shelter for help.

Since the squirrel incident, Bruno (10. stop) _____ walking in Toft Park. He now walks on an indoor track.

B   Unscramble the words to make sentences. Change the verbs in blue into the present perfect.

1. live / since / my family / 2002 / in the same place

    _____

2. love / sing / always / I / to

    _____

3. for / visit / I / want / Paris / a long time / to

    _____

4. a big / friend / pass / exam / just / my

    _____

5. I / one / English / study / year / for

    _____

C   Change the sentences in **B** to make them true for you. Tell a partner.

> My family has lived in the same place since I was born.

5 Writing   **An unusual news story**

A   Read this unusual news story. Then write your own unusual news story.

B   Exchange stories with a partner. Write a headline for your partner's story.

> **STRANGE DRIVER**
>
> Traffic in Sharpville came to a stop yesterday afternoon when a car, without a driver, rolled slowly down Main Street.
> Police are still investigating, but suspect that students from the local university may be behind the trick . . .

6 Communication   **Blogging**

A   Read Melissa's blog entry. What is she writing about? What is her job?

Home	About	Archives	Mail	RSS

Nov 7

Melissa's World
0 Comments | Posted by Melissa

Have you ever read "In the Media" magazine? Well, you should...because I'm going to be in it! I've just finished my interview. I've worked so hard for many years and now my career is going really well. I have two new movies coming out in the fall!

B   Imagine it is ten years from now. You are doing something exciting in your life. Complete these sentences with your own information.

1. I've _____
   for . . . / since . . . _____

2. I've just
   _____

3. Right now I'm
   _____

4. In the future I plan to
   _____

C   On a separate piece of paper, write your own blog entry using the information in **B**. Then follow the steps below.
- Hand in your blog entry.
- Your teacher will shuffle the papers and hand each of you someone else's paper.

> I've worked at this cable news company for two years now. I've just finished my first live broadcast. Right now I'm working in the international news department. In the future I plan to work overseas. I use English in my job and I love it.

D   Get into groups of three. Try to guess whose blog entry you received.

Check out the World Link video.   Practice your English online at http://elt.heinle.com/worldlink

Review: Units 1-3

1 Storyboard

A Talia bought something at a furniture store. She is returning to the store. Look at the pictures and complete the conversations. More than one answer is possible for each blank.

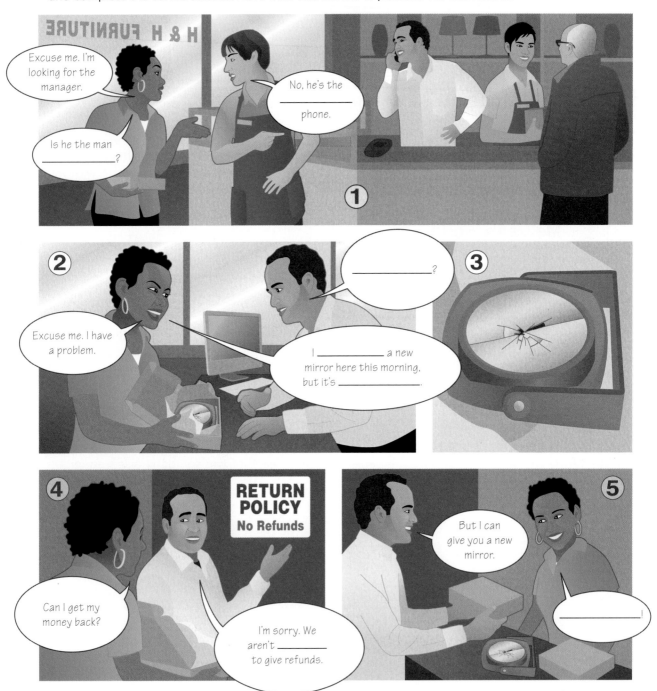

 B Practice the conversation in groups of three. Then change roles and practice again.

2 See It and Say It

 A Look at the picture below. Answer the questions with a partner.
- Where are these people?
- What are they doing? Why are they doing it?

> Daisuke is thinking about buying a houseboat. He wants to live on the water. He'll probably become an artist.

 B With a partner, describe what each person is planning to do in the future. Say as much as you can about each person's plans.

 C Tell a new partner what you plan to do in the future. Where do you plan to live? What kind of work do you plan to do?

3 *Get* and *Have*

A Follow the steps below.

1. Match the words in A, B, and C to make expressions with *get* and *have*.

2. Write your answers in the chart below.

3. Use the column letters (A, B, and C) in the chart as clues to help you.

A	B	C
get have	a children divorced into married your	an argument friendly chat happy childhood news

Get	Have
(A + B) _____ get divorced _____	(A + B) _____
(A + B) _____	(A + B + C) _____
(A + B + C) _____	(A + B + C) _____
(A + B + C) _____	(A + C) _____

B Compare your answers with a partner.

C Take turns choosing an expression in **B**. Make a sentence using that expression.

4 Listening

CD 1
Track 18

A Listen as John and Amy talk about a photo. Use the names in the box to label the people in the picture.

~~John~~	Joseph
Olivia	Randy
Tina	Tom

B Listen again. Complete the chart about where the people are now.

CD 1
Track 18

Joseph and Olivia	They are _____ now. Olivia lives in _____. Joseph is _____ in Florida.
Randy	He just had _____.
Tom	He just _____.
Tina	She's _____ high school.

C Do you have a picture of family members in your wallet or bag? Show your picture to the class and talk about it.

> The person standing in front of me is my sister. Her name is . . .

5 Swimming pool rules

A Look at the picture. Take turns telling the rules at the swimming pool. Point to the people breaking the rules. What are they doing?

B Make up a list of rules for your classroom and share them with the class.

4 Men and Women

Lesson A   How do I look?

1   Vocabulary Link   I like to wear bright colors.

A   Complete the sentences with the correct form of the verbs in the box. (One verb is extra.)

> do   get   wear

1. I like to _____ bright colors. I don't usually _____ makeup and the only time I _____ a skirt is at school—because I have to. My parents aren't too happy about that.

2. I _____ my ears pierced when I was a little girl. I _____ a haircut once a month. One time I even _____ a manicure! Some of my friends are _____ tattoos, but I don't want to.

B   Use your dictionary to look up any unfamiliar words. Then match the verbs with as many nouns as possible. Make a list on a separate piece of paper.

> brush
> chip
> color   your
> straighten
> wash
>
>   face
>   hair
>   nail(s)
>   tooth/teeth

C   Discuss these questions with a partner.

1. Which of the activities in **A** and **B** have you tried?
2. Which ones do you do often? occasionally?
3. What is one activity you would like to try? Which one(s) would you never do?
4. Which ones are appropriate for men only? for women only? for both men and women?

> I think it's OK for both men and women to wear bright colors.

> Yeah, in the summer...at the beach.

2 Listening   Say "cheese"!

A Complete this chart. Then share the information with a partner.

What is the last photo you took?	
Where were you?	
Who were you with?	

CD 1
Track 19

B Listen to the first part of an interview. Complete the sentence below.

Tammy is going to explain how to _____.

a. take better photos of other people

b. look good when someone takes your photo

c. use a digital camera

CD 1
Track 20

C Listen to the entire interview. Complete the sentences with Tammy's advice.

1. Don't wear bright _____ or crazy _____.

2. Wash _____.

3. You can wear _____, but not _____.

4. Brush _____.

5. _____ straight.

6. _____ naturally.

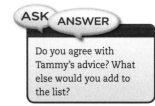

ASK ANSWER

Do you agree with Tammy's advice? What else would you add to the list?

D Take turns telling a partner about Tammy's advice. Use your notes in **C** for support.

3 Pronunciation   Different ways to say *ch*

CD 1
Track 21

A Listen to these sentences. How is the *ch* sound pronounced in each of the underlined words?

1. Say, "cheese"!   2. He works as a chef.   3. I have a headache.

CD 1
Track 22

B Read these items. How is the *ch* sound pronounced in the underlined words? Check (✓) your answers. Then listen and check your answers.

Does it sound like...	cheese?	chef?	headache?
1. I'm studying Chinese.			
2. I sing in the chorus at school.			
3. My brother has a mustache and a beard.			
4. My mother works as an architect.			
5. Have you ever been to Chicago?			
6. He's my high school swimming coach.			
7. ATM stands for "automated teller machine."			

4 Speaking — I'm getting a tattoo!

CD 1 Track 23

A Listen to Chris and Tyler's conversation. Why does Chris want a tattoo? How does he feel and why does he feel that way? How does Tyler feel?

Chris: Guess what? I'm getting a tattoo . . . right here on my right arm!

Tyler: Really? . . . Are you sure?

Chris: Yeah. My best friend has one. It's really cool. Now I want one.

Tyler: But what do your parents think? Did they say anything?

Chris: They're not too happy . . . But I know it's going to look great!

Tyler: I see what you're saying, but . . .

Chris: And I found a really good tattoo artist.

Tyler: But what about the cost? Isn't it expensive?

Chris: No, it's not too bad—and I can pay half now and the rest later.

Tyler: Yeah, but what if you don't like it?

Chris: Don't worry . . . It's going to look great!

B Brainstorm reasons for and against getting a tattoo. Then practice the conversation with a partner.

5 Speaking Strategy

Useful Expressions: Disagreeing politely	
I agree up to a point.	I'm not sure it's / that's (such) a good idea.
Yes, but . . . / I know, but . . .	I see what you're saying, but . . .
I'm not sure. / I don't know.	But what about . . . ?

A Student A is planning to make a change in his or her appearance. Choose one of the ideas below (or one of your own). Role play the situation. Then switch roles.

Student A: Tell your partner about your change. Give reasons why you want to do it.

Student B: Listen to your partner. Politely disagree. Use the Useful Expressions.

shave your head

dye your hair

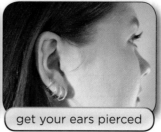

get your ears pierced

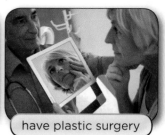

have plastic surgery

Guess what? I'm getting my ears pierced.

Are you serious? Why?

I think it'll look cool.

I'm not so sure . . . Isn't it painful?

6 Language Link   The present perfect with *already*, *just*, *never*, *still*, and *yet*

A   On June 16, Joon asked his girlfriend to marry him. She said *yes*.
Read her diary entries for June 17 and September 20. Study the sentences.

> **June 17**
> Joon and I have **just** gotten engaged. I have **already** told my best friend the good news. I haven't told my parents **yet**. But I will very soon.

> **September 20**
> The wedding plans are moving forward. Joon and I have sent the invitations **already**. I'm nervous. I **still** haven't bought my wedding dress.

B   Complete the statements with the words in bold in **A**.

> 1. You can use _____ and _____ with affirmative verbs in the present perfect.
>
> 2. You can use _____ and _____ with negative verbs in the present perfect.
>
> 3. _____ can be placed in the middle or at the end of a sentence.

C   Read the two conversations. Add the adverb in parentheses to the sentences that precede them. Then practice the conversations with a partner.

February 2

Bob: Hey, Colin. What's wrong?

Colin: It's Sally. She hasn't called. (still)
I gave her my phone number two days ago.

Bob: Be patient! You've met her. (just)

One month later

Bob: Has Sally called? (yet)

Colin: Yes. We've gone on six dates. (already)

Bob: That's great!

Colin: Yeah. And I've asked her to meet my parents! (already)

D   Circle the sentence that best follows the first sentence.

1. He's never worn bright colors.
   a. He's adventurous.
   b. He's not a risk-taker.

2. I've just met Paula.
   a. She's nice.
   b. She's an old friend.

3. I've already gotten a tattoo.
   a. Should I do it?
   b. I really like it!

4. I haven't washed my hair yet.
   a. I'd better hurry.
   b. It looks much better.

5. We still haven't met Sammy.
   a. Will he be at the party?
   b. He's a friendly guy!

6. I haven't seen the doctor yet.
   a. I saw him yesterday.
   b. I'm seeing him later.

7 Communication **Act like a man**

A Read these statements. Check (✓) if you *agree*, *disagree*, or are *not sure*.

Statements about men and women	agree	disagree	not sure
1. Older men and women shouldn't wear bright colors.			
2. For a woman, how much money a man has is more important than his looks.			
3. Men should never wear makeup.			
4. Women shouldn't get tattoos.			
5. Men worry about their appearance as much as women do.			
6. Women should always wear a skirt in formal settings.			
7. Men are first attracted to women because of their appearance.			
8. Athletic women are not attractive to men.			

B Work with three other students. Compare and explain your answers from **A**. If one or more group members disagreed or was not sure, check (✓) the box of that item below.

1. ☐   5. ☐
2. ☐   6. ☐
3. ☐   7. ☐
4. ☐   8. ☐

> I checked "agree" for number 1. I just don't think older people look good in bright colors.

> I know, but some older people like to wear bright colors and I think it's OK. I checked "disagree."

C As a group, work on each statement you checked in **B**. Rewrite the statement so that *everyone* agrees with it.

D Present your group's statements to the class.

ASK ANSWER

Do you think men and women have changed over the years?
If so, how have they changed? If not, why haven't they changed?

Men and Women

Lesson B Dating

1 Vocabulary Link   A love story?

A Read the story. Match the definitions below with the verbs in blue.

a. ____ liked each other

b. ____ invited

c. ____ refused

d. ____ stopped dating

e. ____ became an adult

f. ____ spend time with; date

g. ____ met unexpectedly

h. ____ secretly dated another person

i. ____ stop thinking about

j. ____ started

Gus liked Erin. One day he **(1)** asked her out on a date. Erin was shy. At first she **(2)** turned Gus down.

Gus asked Erin again and she said yes. She agreed to **(3)** go out with him.

They enjoyed spending time together. They **(4)** got along well.

Unfortunately, Gus **(5)** cheated on Erin. She saw him with another girl.

Erin was very upset. She **(6)** broke up with Gus. They stopped dating.

Gus couldn't stop thinking about Erin. He couldn't **(7)** get over her.

Erin and Gus **(8)** grew up and got jobs: Erin worked as a banker and Gus was a newscaster.

They lived in the same city but never **(9)** ran into each other.

One day Erin **(10)** turned on the TV and saw Gus. She decided to call him . . .

B How do you think the story ended? Complete the sentence and finish the story with a partner.

Gus felt _____ when he got Erin's phone call. He . . .

C Tell another pair your story.

2 Listening — I want to go out with him.

CD 1
Track 24

A Alex and Karen are talking about Gabe. Listen and write down the relationships. Use the words in the box. One word is extra.

> I met him before, but at the party he <u>pretended</u> he didn't know me.
>
> What does "pretended" mean? Have you ever pretended not to know someone?

| brothers | friends | classmates | teammates |

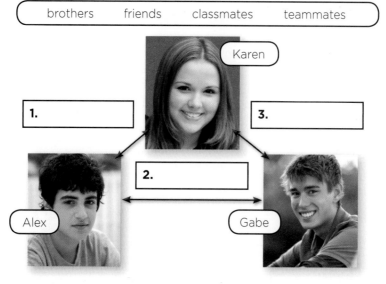

Karen

1. _____

3. _____

2. _____

Alex

Gabe

CD 1
Track 25

B Listen. Complete the flow chart with the missing words.

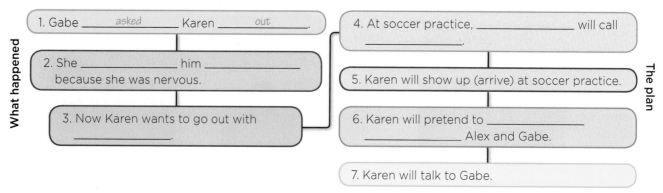

What happened

1. Gabe ___*asked*___ Karen ___*out*___.

2. She _____ him _____ because she was nervous.

3. Now Karen wants to go out with _____.

The plan

4. At soccer practice, _____ will call _____.

5. Karen will show up (arrive) at soccer practice.

6. Karen will pretend to _____ _____ Alex and Gabe.

7. Karen will talk to Gabe.

C Don't look back at your answers in **A** and **B**. Try to answer these questions with a partner.

1. How do Alex, Karen, and Gabe know each other?

2. What happened to Karen?

3. What is her plan now? Do you think it will work? Why or why not?

3 Reading — Ways to meet people

A How do you meet someone special? Answer the questions. Share your answers with a partner.

1. Where is the best place to meet someone?
   - ☐ at school
   - ☐ at a party
   - ☐ your idea: _____

2. What is the best way to meet someone?
   - ☐ have a friend introduce you
   - ☐ wait and be approached by the person
   - ☐ your idea: _____

DATING AROUND THE WORLD

Do you want to go on a date? Are you still single?
So are these people! We asked them two questions:

Q1: How did you recently meet someone?

Q2: How would you like to meet someone?

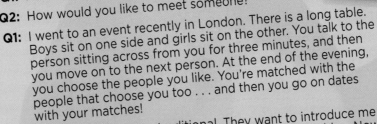

Mahesh, London

Q1: I went to an event recently in London. There is a long table. Boys sit on one side and girls sit on the other. You talk to the person sitting across from you for three minutes, and then you move on to the next person. At the end of the evening, you choose the people you like. You're matched with the people that choose you too . . . and then you go on dates with your matches!

Q2: My parents are more traditional. They want to introduce me to a nice girl. When I was younger, I didn't like the idea. Now I think I might give it a try.

Q1: I ran into this guy I knew from my college days. We went out on a couple of dates. He was nice. We had good conversation and got along OK, but there was no romantic spark.

Q2: It's more relaxing to go out in a big group. I want to meet someone when I'm out with a group of friends. That feels more natural and not so stressful.

Nina, Mexico City

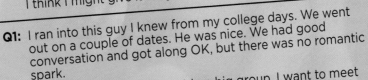

Kaleo, Honolulu

Q1: I met a woman at work. I asked her out, but she turned me down. My friend says it's not good to date people you work with. I think he's probably right.

Q2: I love waterskiing and surfing. I heard that Internet dating is fun. You can read all about the other people and their interests before you contact them. That might work for me.

Q1: I went to a kind of "matchmaking party." There is the same number of boys and girls at the party. It's not very romantic. And when I attended, the drinks were very expensive! Even so, I did match with one guy and we went out the next weekend.

Q2: I'd like to meet someone by myself in a romantic way. Imagine this: there is a huge rainstorm. A handsome stranger shares his umbrella with you. You and he fall in love. I know it sounds crazy, but that's my fantasy.

Fumiko, Osaka

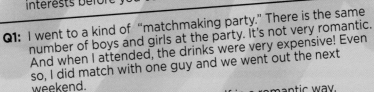

	Yes	No	NM
1. Mahesh			
2. Nina			
3. Kaleo			
4. Fumiko			

B Read each person's response to **Q1**. Did he or she go out on a date? Check (✓) *Yes, No,* or *NM* (not mentioned).

C Read each person's response to **Q2**. Then read the statements below. Which person do you think would say each one? Write his or her name. (There is one extra statement not said by anyone.)

1. I can be shy, so dating one-on-one is hard. _____

2. I'm more of a dreamer than a realist. _____

3. I think looks are not the most important thing. _____

4. I'm open to meeting someone my mom and dad know. _____

5. I want to meet someone who enjoys what I like to do. _____

ASK ANSWER

Would you try any of the dating methods mentioned in this reading? Why or why not?

4 Language Link   Phrasal verbs

A Study the information in the chart. Then read the sentences below. In each group of sentences, which one is wrong? Why? Tell a partner.

Phrasal verbs		
	with an object	**without an object**
separable	Gus asked out <u>Erin</u>. / Gus asked <u>Erin</u> out. ~~Gus asked out her.~~ / Gus asked <u>her</u> out.	I grew up in Taipei. How often do you work out?
inseparable	Gus ran into <u>Erin</u>. Gus ran into <u>her</u>.	The elevator broke down. Please take the stairs.
A phrasal verb = verb + preposition / particle. They are also called two- (or three) word verbs. Some phrasal verbs can be "separated" by a noun or a pronoun.		

1a. Ann likes Bob, so she asked him out.

1b. Ann likes Bob, but she asked Stu out instead.

1c. Ann likes Bob, so she asked out him.

2a. I ran into Sara at the store.

2b. I ran into her at the store.

2c. I ran her into at the store.

B Read Antonio's blog entry. Look at the highlighted words. Classify the different kinds of phrasal verbs. Then explain in your own words what happened to Antonio.

phrasal verbs that can take an object		phrasal verbs without an object
separable	inseparable	
hung up,	get over	catch up, get along,

Home **About** **Archives** **Mail** **RSS**

AUG 10 **ANTONIO'S BLOG**   current mood: ☹

Hey Everyone,

What a day! So . . . I called my girlfriend. I wanted to catch up with her—I hadn't seen her in days. Usually we get along with each other, but today something was different. She sounded upset.

"I saw you yesterday going out with another girl," she said. "I want to break up with you." Then she hung up the phone! I tried to call her back, but she wouldn't pick up the phone. Who was the mysterious "other girl?" My cousin!

I decided to go to the gym and work out. On the way there, my car broke down. Later that day, I wanted to relax, so I turned the TV on. There was no picture. The TV was broken.

I have to get over my terrible day. I don't know what to do. I can't figure it out . . .

C Ask and answer these questions with a partner. Use phrasal verbs.

1. What is the first thing you turn on when you get home?

2. Think about the last test you took. Could you figure out all the answers?

3. Do you work out? Why or why not?

4. Who called you today? Who do you need to call back?

5. When you feel sad, what do you do to get over the feeling?

6. Who do you get along with best in your family?

5 Writing **A personal ad**

A Write your own personal ad. Use the questions below to help you.

What do you do?
What do you do in your free time?
How would you describe your personality?
What are you looking for in another person?

Do you like to travel?

Busy student seeks travel partner during summer vacation. Looking for curious people. Let's explore the world together! I'm fun-loving and easy to get along with.

You should be friendly and athletic.

B Exchange papers with a partner.
Make suggestions that you think will improve your partner's ad.

6 Communication **Dating Survey**

A Complete this dating survey.

Dating Survey

1. Which of these dating methods have you already tried or would you like to try?
   a. Internet dating
   b. personal ads
   c. going on a date with another couple
   d. going on a blind date*
   e. _____

2. The best way to attract someone is to
   a. be friendly
   b. compliment them
   c. act shy
   d. not do anything special
   e. _____

3. What *first* attracts you to a person?
   a. looks
   b. personality
   c. intelligence
   d. having common interests
   e. _____

4. How do you know you really like someone?
   a. My heart beats faster around the person.
   b. I can't stop thinking about the person.
   c. I have a dream about the person.
   d. I can relax around the person.
   e. _____

5. Your boyfriend or girlfriend has cheated on you. What do you do?
   a. break up
   b. ignore it
   c. talk to him or her
   d. wait for him or her to talk to me
   e. _____

6. What should you definitely do on a first date?
   a. bring a gift
   b. talk a lot
   c. offer to split the bill
   d. dress up
   e. _____

7. In a difficult situation, how would you break up with someone?
   a. over the telephone
   b. by e-mail or text message
   c. face-to-face
   d. by ignoring the person
   e. _____

8. Which is the *worst* dating situation?
   a. Your date shows up an hour late.
   b. Your date complains about his or her last date.
   c. Your date doesn't have enough money.
   d. Your date doesn't dress attractively.
   e. _____

*blind date = a romantic date with someone you've never met before

B Compare your answers with a partner.
Which answers were different? Explain your answers.

 Check out the World Link video.   Practice your English online at http://elt.heinle.com/worldlink

Lesson A   Mind your manners

1   Vocabulary Link   Good or bad behavior

A   Meg is talking about her friends and family. Read the sentences. Match the words in blue to their definitions below. What do you think of Meg's opinions? Tell a partner.

> Is it good behavior or bad behavior?

> My classmate found some money on the floor. He picked it up and kept it. Do you think his behavior was (1) inappropriate? Personally, I don't think it was the (2) honest thing to do.

> My grandmother says that kids today are sometimes (3) inconsiderate—that we're selfish. All I know is that I always try to be (4) respectful to my grandparents.

> My friend is always talking on her cell phone when we're hanging out with friends. It really bugs me—I think it's kind of (5) impolite.

> My mom is always telling me to be (6) kind to my little sister. Her behavior can be so (7) unpleasant, but when we're at school I do feel (8) responsible for her.

a. rude ____

b. not caring about other people's feelings ____

c. truthful ____

d. not enjoyable ____

e. in charge of someone/something ____

f. not right for a particular situation ____

g. helpful and caring towards others ____

h. showing politeness towards others ____

B   Complete the chart of opposites with the words in blue from **A**.

| appropriate |
| considerate |
| dishonest |
| disrespectful |
| irresponsible |
| pleasant |
| polite |
| unkind |

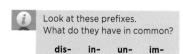
Look at these prefixes. What do they have in common?

dis-   in-   un-   im-

C   You are going to a party. How would you describe these behaviors? Use the words in blue.

- giving a dinner guest the best seat at the table
- chewing gum loudly in public
- arriving ten minutes late to a friend's party
- bringing a small gift to a dinner party

2 Listening **Here are the rules.**

CD 1
Track 26

A Listen. Complete the sentences.

1. The speaker is talking to a group of _____.
2. She works at a _____.

B Look at your answer for **A2**. This place has many different rules that visitors must follow. Can you guess what some of these rules are?

_____

_____

_____

_____

CD 1
Track 27

C Read the sentences below. Then listen to the rules. Choose the best paraphrase for each rule that you hear.

1. a. You must stay on the green and red paths.
   b. Always stay on the red path. You can leave the green path.

2. a. You cannot watch the staff feeding the animals.
   b. Feeding time is open to the public.

3. a. Running or making noise is not allowed anywhere.
   b. Running or making noise is only permitted in certain areas.

4. a. Birds walk freely around some areas. Please don't touch them.
   b. Birds walk freely around some areas. It's OK to touch them.

5. a. You're not allowed to eat lunch inside this place.
   b. You can enjoy lunch inside this place.

6. a. If you don't know what's recyclable, just ask.
   b. Everything goes into the recycle containers.

3 Pronunciation **Linking the same sounds**

A Mari recently had dinner at a nice restaurant. Take turns reading about her experiences aloud. Notice the consonant sounds in blue.

 Notice!
Say these consonant sounds as one long sound. You don't need to say each sound twice.

> Tom, Sue, and I had dinner together. The waiter was polite and considerate. I had the most delicious soup. Tom's steak came out quickly and it was perfectly cooked. We all loved the place. We left twenty dollars for a tip. I would definitely eat there again. In fact, Tom might go there again tonight!

ASK ANSWER

Have you ever been to a place like this? If so, what was it like? If not, would you like to go?

CD 1
Track 28

B Now listen to the story in **A** and practice saying it with a partner. Pay attention to the linked consonant sounds.

4 Speaking — Mmm. It's delicious.

CD 1
Track 29

A Read Ahmed and Inez's conversation. Why are people going to Ahmed's house? What custom is Inez unsure about?

Inez: Wow! Everything smells delicious, Ahmed. How long did it take you to cook all this?

Ahmed: A few hours. But don't worry—I like to cook for my friends. And I like to have dinner parties. Please . . . sit down.

Inez: Um, can I sit anywhere?

Ahmed: Sure. You're the first guest to arrive. Make yourself comfortable.

Inez: You know, I've never had Turkish food before.

Ahmed: Don't worry. I'll explain everything . . . Uh, here, try this.

Inez: Um, is it OK if I use my fingers?

Ahmed: Sure, go right ahead. So, what do you think?

Inez: Mmm. It's delicious.

B Practice the conversation with a partner.

5 Speaking Strategy

A Study the expressions in the Useful Expressions box. Which responses are positive? Which ones are negative? Then read the rules for the two situations below.

Useful Expressions: Asking about customs	

Is it OK to use my fingers?
Is it OK if I use my fingers?
    Please, go right ahead. / Absolutely.
    Actually, it's probably better to use a fork.
    Normally, people use a fork.
	Is it all right to wear shoes inside?
	Is it all right if I wear shoes inside?
	    Sure, no problem. / Yeah, it's fine.
	    Actually, it's best to remove your shoes.
	    No, you really should take off your shoes.

Rules for visiting a mosque	
wear shoes inside	☹
wear shorts	☹
cover your head	☺
sit in a mixed group of men and women	☹

Rules for a formal Japanese dinner	
help yourself to a drink	☹
make special food requests	☹
ask for a knife and fork	☺
leave a tip	☹

B Role play one of the situations above with a partner. One person asks about the customs. The other person explains them. Then switch roles and role play the other situation.

> Is it appropriate to ask for a knife and fork? I can't use chopsticks.

> Absolutely. That's no problem at all.

6 Language Link   *It + be* + adjective + infinitive; gerund as subject

A   Study the two structures in the box. (They have the same meaning.)
Then underline examples of the target structures below.

It + be + adjective + infinitive	Gerund as subject
It's impolite to talk with food in your mouth.	Talking with food in your mouth is impolite.

1. Having bread with your meal is typical in France.

2. It's impolite to ask someone's age in North America.

3. Holding hands in public is inappropriate in Myanmar.

4. It's customary to shake hands when you meet someone in Kenya.

5. It's irresponsible to be 15 minutes late for an appointment in Switzerland.

6. Tipping taxi drivers is unnecessary in Finland.

B   Rewrite the underlined sentences in a different way.

1. *It's typical to have bread with your meal in France.* _____

2. _____

3. _____

4. _____

5. _____

6. _____

C   Look at the customs in **A**. Are they the same in your country?
If not, how are they different? Tell a partner.

> Having bread with your meal isn't typical here.

> Yeah, we usually have rice, not bread.

D   Work with a partner. Think about the customs where you live.
Complete these sentences. Share your ideas with another pair.

It's impolite to ask . . .
It's customary to . . . when you visit someone's home.
. . . is considered rude behavior.

7 Communication   Subway rules

A Study the people in the subway scene below. What are they doing?
Use the words in the box and make sentences about their behavior.

> One woman is eating ice cream on the subway. I think it's inappropriate because . . .

(im)polite   (in)appropriate   (in)considerate   (un)kind

 B You are going to design a poster. Read the information below and look at the examples. Work as a group and draw your poster on a separate piece of paper.

- The city is launching a public awareness campaign for buses and subways.
- Officials are asking riders to design a poster for the campaign.
- The winners will each receive a free one-year bus and subway pass!

 C Put up your posters around the room.
Vote for the best one.

Being Different

Lesson B   Adjusting to a new place

1   Vocabulary Link   Cross-cultural communication

A   Think of a popular travel destination outside of your country. What is one thing that is culturally different about that place? Compare your idea with others in the class.

B   Match the words in columns A and B to make common English expressions. Then match the expressions to their definitions below. Use the underlined words as clues to help you.

A				B			
body	eye	jet	personal	barrier	expression	lag	space
eating	facial	language	small	contact	habits	language	talk

1. <u>words</u> that <u>prevent you from understanding</u> another person   <u>   language barrier   </u>

2. feeling <u>tired</u> after a long <u>airplane</u> trip   <u>   lag   </u>

3. describing <u>how or why</u> people <u>eat</u>   <u>   </u>

4. the <u>look</u> on a person's <u>face</u> (for example, smiling)   <u>   </u>

5. <u>conversation</u> about <u>unimportant</u> or everyday things   <u>   small   </u>

6. <u>directly looking at</u> another person's <u>eyes</u>   <u>   </u>

7. an imaginary <u>area</u> around each <u>person</u>   <u>   </u>

8. <u>communication</u> through how we move our <u>bodies</u>   <u>   </u>

C   Imagine you are traveling to another country. Read these Travel Tips from a guidebook. Use the expressions in **B** to complete the sentences. Compare your answers with a partner.

On the plane, change your watch to match the time of your destination city. Change your (1)_____ (when you take your meals) to follow the new time. Doing this may help you avoid a bad case of (2) _____.

It's hard to know how to break through the (3) _____ when you don't speak the language well. Smile and try your best. You can make (4) _____ with the locals as a first step by talking about the weather, and things to do and see. When you're making conversation, be respectful of others' (5) _____. You don't want to stand too close!

Learn about (6) _____—how you move your arms and legs communicates a lot! For example, making direct (7) _____ can be inappropriate in some cultures. People think it's rude. Also, certain (8) _____, such as smiling, can have different meanings, so be careful.

D   Complete these sentences. Then compare your answers with a partner.

1. The best way to avoid jet lag is . . .

2. You can overcome a language barrier by . . .

3. When I make small talk, I talk about . . .

2 Listening We've been talking about . . .

CD 1
Track 30

A You will hear three selections from different lectures. What is each lecture about? Listen and match the topic to the lecture. (You will only use half the topics.)

> a. body language   c. eye contact   e. personal space
> b. eating habits   d. jet lag   f. small talk

Lecture #1: _____   Lecture #2: _____   Lecture #3: _____

CD 1
Track 30

B Before you listen, write in the topic (from **A**) for each lecture. Then listen and complete the notes below. Write only one or two words per blank.

Lecture #1: _____

I. Conversations about _____ things

II. Popular topics:

    1) _____

    2) _____*and*_____

    3) _*shared experiences*_

Lecture #2: _____

I. You can understand a person just by _____ him or her.

    1. Communication:

      a)_____% : the words we use

      b)_____%: the way our _____

Lecture #3: _____

I. How to make a good _____

    1. DO

      a. _____ at the person

    2. DON'T

      a. _____ at someone because the person will feel _____

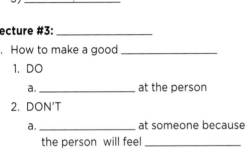

3 Reading JT's Travel Blog

A Imagine that you had to live away from home for six months. What would you miss the most? Tell a partner.

B JT spent six months studying overseas. Read some of his blog entries on page 53.
Next to each date, write *H* if JT was happy on that day, or *U* if he was unhappy.

July 14 _____   September 18 _____   November 23 _____

August 1 _____   October 31 _____   November 27 _____

C Look at the chart below. Notice how the words in blue were used in phrases on page 51. How are they used on page 53? Scan the reading and write your answers. Then answer the questions with a partner.

- Do the two phrases mean the same thing or something different?

- If they are different, how?

Vocabulary Link	Reading
avoid a bad case of jet lag	I was jet lagged.
make direct eye contact	
break through the language barrier	
change your eating habits	
make small talk	

JUL 14 JT's World

I've been here about a month. It's harder than I thought. At first, I was jet lagged. I had less energy and I slept all the time. When I felt better, I noticed something: everyone seemed to avoid making eye contact with me. Is it me—or some kind of cultural difference?

AUG 1 JT's World

I'm a little discouraged. I don't know if I will ever overcome the language barrier here. I try to communicate with gestures and facial expressions. Unfortunately, it doesn't usually work very well.

Uh…jina…um…lako…nani?

???

SEP 18 JT's World

Yesterday I went to the movies wth some friends. Afterwards, we went out to dinner. It was really fun! People don't eat much junk food here, so I'm able to break some of my bad eating habits. I'm actually getting healthier by being here!

OCT 31 JT's World

Tomorrow is my birthday, but I won't be celebrating. I've been sick for about a week. And I feel homesick. I miss my friends and family. People here are nice, but they don't really know me. Sometimes I feel like I'm pretending to be someone else.

NOV 23 JT's World

Tomorrow I go home! It was difficult to live here at first, but now I love it and I don't want to leave yet. Anyway, it's been a great experience and I can't wait to tell everyone about it in person!

I had a great trip!

Uh huh…I see…

NOV 27 JT's World

Well, I'm at home, but it doesn't feel like home. No one seems very interested in my experiences overseas. My friends just want to engage in small talk. It seems so unimportant. Have I changed or has this place changed?

ASK ANSWER

What was the hardest thing for JT to adjust to? What would be the hardest thing for you?

D   What do you think happened next? Write a blog entry of two or three sentences for January 20. Exchange your blog with a partner.

4 Language Link   **Future time clauses**

 A   Study the information in the chart and complete the sentences in the box with the correct answers. Then change one of the clauses in each speech bubble to make it true for you. Tell a partner.

Main clause	Time clause
I'll have to study hard I'm going to take a big trip I'll probably move out	<u>before</u> I take the TOEFL exam. <u>once</u> I graduate from college. <u>when</u> I get accepted to college.
Time clause	**Main clause**
<u>After</u> I get a job, <u>As soon as</u> the weather warms up,	I'll find my own apartment. I'm going to the beach.

1. The main clause uses a future / present verb form.

2. The time clause is usually in the simple present / simple past.

> I'll probably get married when I'm 24.

> After I get a job, I'll buy a new car.

 B   Look at the sentences in **A** again. Which event happens first?
On a separate piece of paper, write your answers.
Check your answers with a partner.

I'll have to study hard before I take the TOEFL exam.

First I will study hard. Then I will take the TOEFL exam.

 C   Alejandro is planning to attend the University of Southern California (USC). Look at his timeline. Then use the words in parentheses to connect the phrases and make sentences about the future.

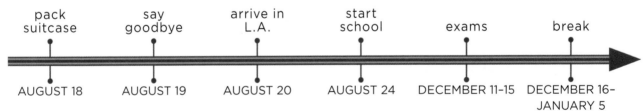

pack suitcase	say goodbye	arrive in L.A.	start school	exams	break
AUGUST 18	AUGUST 19	AUGUST 20	AUGUST 24	DECEMBER 11–15	DECEMBER 16–JANUARY 5

1. pack his suitcase / say goodbye to his friends (before)

_____

2. start winter break / finish his final exams (as soon as)

_____

3. arrive in Los Angeles / start school (four days after)

_____

4. get accepted to USC / move to Los Angeles (when)

_____

5. take his final exams / finish his classes (once)

_____

5 Writing · A language barrier

A Imagine you want to communicate with someone who doesn't speak your language well. What strategies can you use? Add three ideas to the list below.

speak very slowly _____   _____

_____   _____

B Write about ways to overcome a language barrier. Use the ideas listed in **A**.

OVERCOMING A LANGUAGE BARRIER

When you can't communicate in the same language easily, it's important to speak slowly. You don't have to speak louder, just more clearly. You can also draw pictures. For example, I use pictures . . .

C Exchange papers with a partner. Rank your partner's ideas from most to least effective.

6 Communication · Help for the homesick

A Read about these four people's difficulties living abroad. What advice would you give each person?

"At home I'm very independent, but I don't know the customs here, so I'm kind of shy."

– Russell in Europe

"I studied before I came here, but I can't communicate with anyone very well. I don't know how to improve my language skills."

– Julia in Africa

"People here are nice, but I'm homesick. I miss my family and friends."

– Clara in North America

"I like the food here, but I can only order two or three dishes, so I'm always eating the same thing!"

– Chris in Asia

B Read the list of advice for people who are having difficulties. Add your own ideas to the list.

1. Get away. Take a little trip.
2. Go to the movies.
3. Take a cooking class.
4. Invite people to your home.
5. I'd say, "Life at home can be hard, too."
6. Try to talk to little kids.
7. Volunteer somewhere.
8. I'd say, "Your feelings will pass soon."
9. _____
10. _____

C Choose a piece of advice for each person in **A**.

Check out the World Link video.

Practice your English online at http://elt.heinle.com/worldlink

6 Big Business

Lesson A   Success stories

1 Vocabulary Link   Talking about business

A Read the sentences below. How many of the words in blue do you know? What do they mean?
Use your dictionary to help you. Compare your answers with a partner.

1. They plan to advertise their new product on TV and online.

2. If you consume too many calories, you'll gain weight.

3. Since our sales plan isn't working, we'll have to develop a new one.

4. Their company is pretty small. It only employs 20 people.

5. They are looking for someone to invest $2 million in the project.

6. Ms. Park is the head of that department. She manages ten people.

7. What does your company make? It produces batteries for cell phones.

8. My doctor promotes walking as a way to lose weight.

9. Do you want to buy something? To purchase an item, please click on the "buy now" button.

10. Once we receive your money, we'll ship your order to you.

B Now read these bios of three famous companies. Complete the sentences with the verbs from **A**.
(Use the words in parentheses to help you.) Can you guess the names of the companies being
described? Check your answers on page 154.

Worldwide, people (1)_____consume_____ (drink) a lot of coffee every day! Many of those people enjoy this company's bottled coffee products. The company (2)_____ (buys) coffee from farmers and sells it in their stores. It (3)_____ (gives jobs to) 172,000 people worldwide. Some employees are called "baristas"—they work in and (4)_____ (be responsible for running) coffeehouses for the company.

Their first products were running shoes, but now this company (5)_____produces_____ (makes) many different kinds of sports equipment. Today many famous athletes, such as Maria Sharapova and Ronaldinho, (6)_____ (help to make more popular) their products, which are (7)_____ (sent) to more than 45 countries worldwide.

The founders of this company, Larry Page and Sergey Brin, wanted to help people find information on the Internet. They (8)_____developed_____ (designed and made) a search engine to make the process quick and easy. The company makes money when other companies (9)_____ (tell people about) their products online. The company has also (10)_____ (spent) money in many other projects, such as Gmail (an email service).

C Complete the chart with the noun forms of the verbs. Be careful of the spelling!

 Do you know . . . ?

These words also have noun forms ending in *-er/-or* (*consumer, investor*). Which one also has a noun form ending in *-ee*?

Nouns ending in *-ment*				Nouns ending in *-tion*	
advertise	*advertisement*	invest		consume	*consumption*
develop		manage		produce	
employ		ship		promote	

2 Listening   **An article about email**

A   Circle the things that you do a lot. Where are you when you do these things?

> send email   chat online   send text messages   talk on my cell phone

B   Read the questions and responses below. Listen and circle the best answer to each question. Then answer the third question.

1. Lian is reading an article. What is the main purpose of the article?

   a. to introduce a new way to email
   b. to describe when we use email
   c. to give tips for using email well
   d. to talk about the future of email

2. What does the article say about the two groups of people?

   a. They have similar habits.
   b. They email all the time.
   c. They send an average of 100 emails a day.
   d. Half of them do one thing, while half do another.

3. Can you describe the two types of emailing behavior? Which describes Arturo? Lian?

C   What *two* reasons does Arturo give to explain his behavior? What about Lian? Listen again and circle your answers.

Arturo	Lian
1. He worries about having too many emails.	1. She thinks balance is important.
2. He loves being on the computer.	2. She wants to do other things.
3. He doesn't have a lot of free time.	3. She gets exhausted.
4. He doesn't like to wait.	4. She prefers to use her cell phone.

ASK ANSWER
Are you more like Arturo or Lian? How so?

3 Pronunciation   **Stress on nouns and verbs with the same spelling**

A   Listen and repeat the following sentences. Note where the stress falls in the underlined words.

NOUN: How many <u>PRE</u>sents did you get on your birthday?

VERB: He pre<u>SENTS</u> his ideas to the board of directors at 2:00.

B   Listen to these sentences.

NOUN	VERB
1.a. Where does your family buy its produce?	b. What does Nokia produce?
2.a. Do you keep a journal or a record of your life?	b. Would you like to record your voice and listen to it?
3.a. What's your address?	b. How do you address your teacher?

C   Ask and answer the questions in **B** with a partner.

4 Speaking   **People first!**

CD 1
Track 34

A   Listen to this interview with a successful businesswoman.

Host: I'd like to welcome Beverly Smith, the CEO for Sound Smart Inc., to our show today . . . Welcome, Beverly! So, my first question is what *does* Sound Smart do exactly?

Beverly: Well, as you know, a lot of people are studying English. And many of them want to be able to study anywhere, so we produce audio books for your iPod . . . Maybe you've seen one of our advertisements online?

Host: Yes, I have. What a great idea—how convenient! Can I get one of your audio books?

Beverly: Sure. After you make a purchase, you can download the book online. It's simple.

Host: What is the main focus of your company?

Beverly: Well, we really believe in our employees. The bottom line is that happy employees make a good product. So our company slogan is "People First!"

Host: How exactly do you do that—put people first?

Beverly: Well, for one thing, we have a lot of perks.* Our company has its own gym in the building. Also, each of our 100 employees gets the day off on his or her birthday.

Host: Nice! Where can I get an application?

* perks = extra things you receive because of your job (for example, extra holidays, etc.)

B   Now cover the conversation in **A** and complete this company profile of Sound Smart with a partner.

Name of company: _____*Sound Smart*_____
Product/Service: _____
Company slogan: _____
Perks: _____
Other: _____

5 Speaking Strategy

A   Work with a partner to create your own company. On a separate piece of paper, make a company profile.

B   You're going to tell another pair of students about your company. Prepare a short presentation. Use the expressions in the box to emphasize certain points.

C   Take turns presenting to another pair. Take notes as you listen. At the end of the presentation, answer this question: Would you like to work for the company you heard about? Why or why not?

> **Useful Expressions**
>
> **Emphasizing important points**
>
> I'd like to emphasize that . . .
>
> Never forget that . . .
>
> This is a key point.
>
> The bottom line is . . .

> Vocabulary in English, Lesson 1

6 Language Link   The passive: simple present and simple past

A Read the sentences about Oktoberfest. How are the active sentences (A) and passive sentences (B) different? What do you notice about the subjects, verbs, and objects? Discuss with a partner.

Subject	Verb	Object	
(A) The king (B) The first Oktoberfest	held was held	the first Oktoberfest (by the king)	in 1810.
(A) People (B) Four million liters of beer	consume are consumed	four million liters of beer (by people)	each year.

B Read this bio of Unilever, the world's largest company. Find and circle six examples of the passive.

- Unilever was created in 1930 by a British soap maker and Dutch margarine producer.
- Today 400 brands of home, personal care, and food products are sold by the company.
- Some of the more popular products are Knorr® (soups), Lipton® (tea), and Dove® (soap).
- Lux®soap, which was introduced in 1924, became the first mass-marketed soap in the world.
- Today Knorr® is Unilever's most popular brand. It is sold in over 80 countries.
- The multinational company operates companies and factories on every continent except Antarctica.
- 174,000 people are employed by the company worldwide.
- 160 million times a day, a Unilever product is purchased by someone—somewhere in the world.

C Now rewrite the passive sentences in **B** as active sentences.

1. In 1930, _____ *a British soap maker and Dutch margarine producer created Unilever.* _____.
2. The company _____.
3. In 1924, a man _____.
4. Today Unilever _____ in over 80 countries.
5. _____ 174,000 people.
6. 160 million times a day, someone in the world _____.

D Read these facts about the global pop music business. Are the sentences active or passive? Write the correct form of each verb in parentheses.

1. Pop music _____(produce) everywhere in the world.
2. One third of all recorded pop music _____(purchase) in the U.S.
3. Each person in the U.K. _____(buy) an average of four CDs a year.
4. About 10% of pop music albums _____(make) money. The other 90% _____(lose) money.
5. Up to 90% of the global music market _____(control) by only five companies.
6. These five companies _____(know) as "the Big Five."
7. No one can _____(predict) the future of the pop music business.

7 Communication **What is made in your country?**

A Look at the map and photos. Then read about Iceland and answer the four questions.

1. Is Iceland a big or small country?
2. Is it hot or cold there?
3. What else do you know about Iceland?
4. How is it different from your country?

Iceland

Population: 320,000
Capital city: Reykjavik
Literacy rate: Almost 100%
Natural wonders: Glaciers, geysers, hot springs
Government: Democracy (the world's oldest)
Animals: Cattle, sheep, polar bears, seabirds
Fruits and vegetables: Turnips, potatoes
Exports: Seafood
Money: Icelandic krona
Languages: Icelandic, English, Nordic languages
Activities: Whale watching, hiking, skiing

100 mi

Arctic Circle

ICELAND

Reykjavik

geyser

Icelandic krona

glacier

polar bears

B With a partner, state the different facts about Iceland. Use active and passive sentences. Use the verbs in the box in your description.

raise (animals, children)
import / export (food, gas, products)
make / produce (cars, electronics)
find / see (natural wonders, wild animals)
grow (fruits, vegetables)
speak (languages)

The population of Iceland is only 320,000.

You can go whale watching in Iceland.

Cattle and sheep are raised there.

WORLD LINK

What word in English comes from the Icelandic language?
a. glacier
b. geyser
c. hot springs

C With a partner, make up a list of facts about your city, region, or country. Use at least three of the verbs from the box in **B**. Present your list of facts to the class.

Big Business

Lesson B The ABCs of advertising

1 Vocabulary Link Up and down

A Study the graph at the right. Then read about advertising and the economy and answer the questions.

Is most of the news positive or negative? How do you know? What is the positive news?

(a) Overall, business is in a slump. Experts expect the situation to get worse before the economy can recover. The poor economy affects advertisers too. Revenue* continues to be down. **(b)** For the last few years, companies have experienced a sharp fall in profits. Newspapers continue to struggle. **(c)** There has been a steady decline in their advertising revenue for the third year in a row. There is one bright spot in the news: **(d)** The number of companies advertising on the Internet has increased dramatically and **(e)** overall consumer spending has risen slightly.

*revenue = income; money earned

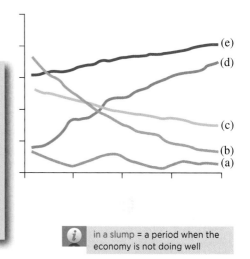

in a slump = a period when the economy is not doing well

B Use some of the words in blue to complete the chart.

	adjectives	adverbs	verbs / nouns
small in amount	slight	_____	(▲) _____, _____
constant, not sudden	gradual, _____	gradually, steadily	(▼) decrease, _____,
large in amount, sudden	dramatic, _____	_____, sharply	_____

C How many of these words do you remember or know? Can you use each one in a sentence?

> recover   get better   get worse   (be) up   (be) down

D Read about these graphs. Then use the words in the box to complete sentences about them. (You will use one of the words twice.)

> decrease   gradual   rose   a slump
> down   increase   slightly   up

1. We've seen a _____ _____ in unemployment, but numbers are still _____.

2. New car sales are in _____. Recently they _____ _____.

3. The number of students studying English is _____ and _____, but overall there has been an _____.

2 Listening · Commercials

A What is a commercial that you can remember? What do you remember most about it (the words, a character, a song)? Tell a partner.

B Listen to these four commercials. What kind of product is being advertised in each one? Write down key words you hear.

CD 1
Track 35

1. _____

   key words: _____

2. _____

   key words: _____

3. _____

   key words: _____

4. _____

   key words: _____

C Listen again. Circle the sentence that best describes the main point of each commerical.

CD 1
Track 35

1. a. First class is the most comfortable.

   b. All customers are treated equally.

   c. Our staff is very special.

2. a. The Candid 100 is slightly more expensive.

   b. The Candid 100 is gradually getting popular.

   c. The Candid 100 is dramatically cheaper.

3. a. Try this and you'll feel better.

   b. Try this after dinner.

   c. Try this when you're cold.

4. a. It's a little expensive, but well made.

   b. It's a big car with good gas mileage.

   c. It's a little car with a lot of room.

ASK ANSWER

You have listened to commercials for four different products or services. Would you buy any or use any of them? What are your favorite products or services?

3 Reading · Is advertising necessary?

A Complete these two statements and then discuss them as a group.

1. There is _____ advertising in our society.
   a. too much   b. just the right amount of

2. Advertising is _____ to sell products.
   a. necessary   b. not necessary

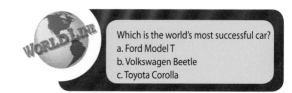

Which is the world's most successful car?
a. Ford Model T
b. Volkswagen Beetle
c. Toyota Corolla

B Read the article below. Compare your answers in **A** with the author's opinion.

Ad or no ad?

Is advertising really necessary? Billions of dollars are spent on it every year, so it must be important. After all, it's a busy world. You have to advertise and get people's attention to sell products!

Not every company thinks that way, however. Despite avoiding traditional ways of advertising, the NO-AD company ("no-ad" stands for "not advertised") has seen a steady increase in their profits over the years. And because their advertising plan is atypical, they can save money and keep costs down. That makes their products more affordable for consumers.

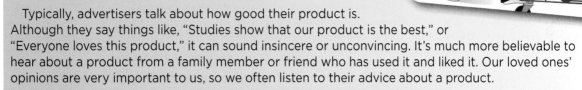

NO-AD sells its products by word of mouth. "Word-of-mouth advertising" happens when one person tells another about a good experience with a product or service. That second person then tells another friend, family member, or colleague. And so a chain of information is created.

Typically, advertisers talk about how good their product is. Although they say things like, "Studies show that our product is the best," or "Everyone loves this product," it can sound insincere or unconvincing. It's much more believable to hear about a product from a family member or friend who has used it and liked it. Our loved ones' opinions are very important to us, so we often listen to their advice about a product.

Word-of-mouth advertising has other advantages, too. It's cost-effective (after all, it's free) and a company doesn't have to create a complex business plan to do it. Here is some advice for small businesses about word-of-mouth advertising:

- Be prepared to talk about your company at any time. You never know who you will meet. Always carry business cards.

- Only say positive things about your company. Don't say negative things about your competition.

- Help other companies by referring people to them. The more you help others, the more good fortune will come back to you . . . and that's good business!

C Scan the reading quickly. Find the opposites of these words. Use your dictionary for any words you don't know.

1. typical ➝ _____
2. simple ➝ _____
3. sincere ➝ _____
4. negative ➝ _____
5. convincing ➝ _____

ASK ANSWER

Do you agree with the advice given for small businesses? Why or why not?

There are many different types of advertising. Which method do you think is best?

D How does word-of-mouth advertising work? How is paid media advertising different? Write down your ideas in the chart below. Compare with a partner.

Word-of-Mouth Advertising	Paid Media Advertising (Radio, TV, etc.)
1. You hear about a product from _____.	1. _____
2. It can sound more _____.	2. _____
3. It doesn't _____ anything—it's _____.	3. _____
4. You don't need _____ to do it.	4. _____

4 Language Link   Connecting words: *because, so, although / even though*

A   Complete the ad below with the connecting words *because*, *so*, and *even though*. What is the ad selling? Why should you buy it?

 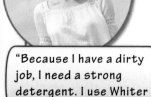
Although and *even though* have the same meaning.

"Although I have a big, messy family, everyone looks clean! Thanks, Whiter & Brighter!"

WHITER & BRIGHTER
LAUNDRY DETERGENT

More people are using new and improved *Whiter & Brighter*
1. _____ it really works!

We know that you love your old brand. Well, it can't beat *Whiter & Brighter* 2. _____ it may do a fairly good job.

Millions of customers are trying it, 3. _____ why don't you try it too!

"Because I have a dirty job, I need a strong detergent. I use Whiter & Brighter!"

B   Use the connecting words to join together these sentences. Which items can you answer in more than one way? Check your answers with a partner.

1. We can't advertise on TV. It's expensive. (because)
2. I hate TV commercials. I don't watch much television. (so)
3. Advertising on TV is very expensive. Companies still do it. (although)
4. You never know who you will meet. You should always carry business cards. (because)
5. It sounded insincere. I listened to their sales pitch. (even though)
6. I decided to try it. My mother liked that shampoo. (so)

C   Which connecting words in **B** . . .

1. introduce a clause that gives a reason? _____
2. introduce a clause that shows a result? _____
3. introduce a clause with a surprising result? _____

D   Complete the sentences below with *although/even though*, *because*, or *so*. Then explain your choices.

1. It was on sale, _____*so*_____ many people bought it.
2. People say word-of-mouth advertising is cost-effective _____ it's free.
3. _____ their product is affordable, it doesn't work as well as ours.
4. The new toy was very popular, _____ all the stores quickly sold out of it.
5. _____ it increases their sales, many companies spend money on advertising.

5 Writing   Consumer advice

A   You have been asked to write a review for a magazine. Choose an item you have bought recently and write about its good and bad qualities.

B   Share your writing with a partner.
Talk about the item's good and bad points.

THIS PRODUCT IS RATED: ☆☆☆☆☆

I like to go mountain biking. When it's hot, I often stop to drink water. I like to use my Hydro-Pak because I can ride and drink at the same time! The Hydro-Pak has a hose connected to a water container inside. It's convenient and lightweight. It comes in many different colors, so I'm sure you can find one you like.

6 Communication   Rate the advertisement.

A   Look at the bike below and read about it. What do you think of this product? Tell your partner.

CITYBIKE MINI

"The Foldable Bike"

Lightweight folding bike

Perfect for city commutes

Fits easily on overhead train racks

B   You and your partner work for an advertising agency. You need to create a magazine ad for the product in **A**. Follow the steps below.

- On a separate piece of paper, create your ad.
- As you create the ad, think about the questions below.

	Yes	No
1. Is the ad eye-catching?	○	○
2. Is the message positive?	○	○
3. Is the design simple and clean?	○	○
4. Is the ad original?	○	○

5. What do you like most about this ad?_____

6. Would you buy this product? Why or why not?_____

_____

C   As a group, choose your favorite ad.

Check out the World Link video.   Practice your English online at http://elt.heinle.com/worldlink

1 Storyboard

A Al is always borrowing things from his friend Manny. Look at the pictures and complete the conversation. More than one answer is possible for each blank.

 B Practice the conversation. Then change roles and practice again.

2 See It and Say It

A Look at these pictures of Bev and Dan and answer the questions. Use some of the verbs from the box in your answers. Work with a partner.

> ask out   catch up   get along   go out   run into   work out

1. Where are Bev and Dan in each picture? What are they doing?
2. In the first picture, what do you think happened? What is Dan saying to Bev?
3. In the second situation, what do you think they are talking about?

B On a separate piece of paper, write a conversation for each situation. Then act the conversations out.

3 The Cultural Iceberg

A Read about the cultural iceberg and some information about Japan. Circle the correct answers.

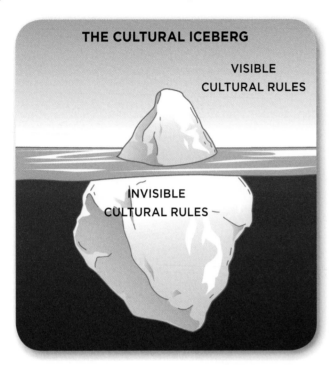

THE CULTURAL ICEBERG

VISIBLE
CULTURAL RULES

INVISIBLE
CULTURAL RULES

Culture is similar to an iceberg. There are cultural rules that are visible and easy to understand. Most of our cultural values, however, are invisible or hidden. For example, when you visit a restaurant in Japan, people may sit on the floor and use chopsticks to eat. These (eating habits / facial expressions) are easy to (come across / figure out). You may not know, however, that while it's (common / uncommon) for men to sit cross-legged on the floor, it's considered (appropriate / inappropriate) for women to do so. You have to study people's (personal space / body language) to understand this less visible cultural rule.

B Now think about your own country. Complete the chart with cultural *dos* and *don'ts* (the rules of behavior) that you think are important.

	eating habits	small talk	body language
Dos			
Don'ts			

C Share your cultural *dos* and *don'ts* with the class.

4 Listening

CD 1
Track 36

You will hear a question or statement and three responses spoken in English.
Select the best response to the question or statement and circle the letter (A, B, C).

1. A   B   C   4. A   B   C
2. A   B   C   5. A   B   C
3. A   B   C   6. A   B   C

5 Communication

A Read these advertising slogans. Complete each one with a word from the box.
Guess with a partner.

beautiful	dreams	driving	flowers
~~milk~~	news	skies	world

1. "Got _____milk_____?"

2. "Say it with _____."

3. "Fly the friendly _____."

4. "All the _____ that's fit to print"

5. "The ultimate _____ machine"

6. "Give us 20 minutes and we'll give you
   the _____."

7. "Easy, breezy, _____ . . . Cover Girl"

8. "Where _____ come true"

B With a partner, look at the slogans in **A** again.
Can you match each one to a company or brand below?

BMW

British Broadcasting Corporation (the BBC)

California Milk Processor Board

Disney World

Florists' Transworld Delivery (FTD)

Cover Girl Cosmetics

The New York Times (newspaper)

United Airlines

C Ask and answer these questions with a partner.

1. What kind of companies are listed in **B**?

2. What do they produce or what service do they offer?

3. Which slogan do you like best? Why? Which slogan promotes its company the best?

4. Which slogan is your least favorite? Why?

5. Imagine you can invest some money in one of these companies.
   Which one would you choose? Which one(s) would you avoid? Why?

7 Health

Lesson A   How do you feel?

1   Vocabulary Link   Adventure on a mountain

A   Read part of a story below. What do the words in blue mean?

This work is making me drowsy.

This ride will make you dizzy.

He shivered with cold.

> ### *Adventure on a Mountain* by Michael Yamato
>
> There were more than twenty climbers on the mountain that day. We had been climbing for hours. My partner, Ed, and I were trying to reach the top before noon.
>
> It was freezing and the winds were strong. We were both wet and cold. Worst of all, a big storm was approaching.
>
> That's when the trouble began. Ed started to get drowsy. He kept saying, "I just want to sleep." He was talking, but I couldn't understand him clearly—he wasn't making sense. The air was very thin and I felt dizzy too, but Ed was *really* confused. His steps were heavy. He was obviously exhausted.
>
> Ed's body was very cold. Then he started to shiver uncontrollably. His breathing was slowing down. I was getting scared. I was tired, too, but suddenly my own weakness disappeared. I needed to help Ed. It was then that I remembered the dry clothes and warm drinks in my backpack . . .

Match the words with their meanings.

1. drowsy ___*e*___   5. shiver _____

2. make sense _____   6. breathe _____

3. dizzy _____   7. weak _____

4. exhausted _____

a. not strong	d. very tired
b. to shake because of cold	e. sleepy
c. to be clear or understandable	f. to take air into your body
	g. unable to balance

B   Now answer these questions about the story. Compare your answers with a partner.

1. Where were Michael and Ed?

2. How did they feel at first?

3. What happened to Ed next?

4. What do you think they should have done? (Give a reason to support your answer.)

   ☐ continued to the top   ☐ waited for help   ☐ turned back

5. How do you think the story ended?

C   Here are some more words about health. (You might hear these sentences in a doctor's office.) Can you match each word in blue with one or more parts of the body on the right?

1. When you take these tablets, don't chew them—just swallow them with some water.

2. Look straight ahead. Try not to blink.

3. Please relax and just breathe normally.

4. Turn your head to the right and cough twice.

chest
eyes
mouth
nose
teeth
throat

2 Listening A cold or the flu?

A Read the definition of the word *symptom*. What are the symptoms of the common cold? How about the flu? Make a list with a partner.

symptom = (n.) a physical change (such as a fever) that is caused by an illness

CD 2
Track 2

B Listen to the first part of this conversation. Circle the correct answer.

1. Susan is a student / teacher / doctor.

2. The man is a student / teacher / patient.

CD 2
Track 3

C Listen. Choose six answers from the box and write the correct letters in the chart. There are three extras.

	Cold	Flu
Fever		typical high fever
Exhaustion		early and severe
Body pain		severe
Sore throat	common	
	mild	can last _____

a. always
b. sometimes
c. never
d. mild
e. severe
f. rare
g. weakness
h. 2-3 days
i. 2-3 weeks

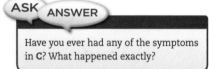

ASK ANSWER

Have you ever had any of the symptoms in **C**? What happened exactly?

3 Pronunciation Dropping the *h*

CD 2
Track 4

A Look at these pictures. Listen to the advice given for each one. Notice how the *h*- sound is dropped when the pronouns are linked to the word before them.

Ed is about to faint.

Stop him from falling.
Ask him to sit down.
Loosen his collar.

Ann has already fainted.

Lay her on her back.
Raise her legs.
Check her body for injuries.

B Practice reading the sentences in **A** with a partner.

C With a partner, choose one of these situations. What should be done? Make a list of advice and read it aloud.

1. You're on a camping trip in the mountains. One of your friends has a bad stomachache.

2. Your class has just ended. Your friend stands up to leave and suddenly feels dizzy.

3. Your 70-year-old neighbor is having trouble breathing.

ADVICE

1. Have her relax.
2. Give her some . . .

4 Speaking   I could never do that.

CD 2
Track 5

A Ming wants to join the school swim team. Before she can do that, she has to get a checkup from her doctor. Listen to the conversation.

   1. Read the conversation. Underline the language the doctor uses to give advice.

   2. Do you think the language is formal or informal?

Dr. Pena: OK, Ming, we're finished. As far as I can tell, you're completely healthy!

Ming: Great!

Dr. Pena: But I do want to talk to you about one thing.

Ming: Uh-oh. This doesn't sound good.

Dr. Pena: No, it's nothing scary. It's just that winter is coming. You need to prepare. I always advise my patients to get a flu shot.

Ming: Hmm . . . I could never do that. I'm afraid of needles!

Dr. Pena: Don't worry, Ming. The shot doesn't hurt at all.

Ming: Really? Well, maybe . . .

Dr. Pena: It will protect you from the flu. You'll be able to swim all year without getting sick. In my opinion, I think you should do it.

Ming: Well, OK. Maybe I'll give it a try.

Dr. Pena: Good! I'll tell the nurse to come in and see you. Take care and good luck on the swim team this year!

B Practice the conversation with a partner.

5 Speaking Strategy

A Look at the two situations.
Work with a partner and answer these questions.

   1. What's happened in each situation?

   2. How does each person feel?

B Choose one of the situations in **A** and write a conversation. Work with your partner.
Student A: You are a helpful person.
Student B: You have the problem.
Use the Useful Expressions to help you.

A: Excuse me. Are you all right?
B: I'm not sure.
A: What happened?
B: I fell off my bike.
A: How do you feel? Are you dizzy?

C Perform your conversation for the class.

Useful Expressions	
Giving serious advice	
In my opinion, you should . . .	I think the best idea (for you) is to . . .
I always advise people to . . .	
	If I were you, I'd . . .
Accepting advice	**Refusing advice**
You're right. Thanks for the advice.	I'm not sure that would work for me.
That makes (a lot of) sense. I'll give it a try.	That doesn't (really) make sense to me.
I'll try it and get back to you.	I could never do that.

6 Language Link   Verb + noun / adjective / verb(-ing); noun + hurt(s)

A Study the expressions in the chart. Then look at the words in the box on the right. Where do they fit in the chart? Can you think of any other nouns, adjectives, or verbs to put in the chart?

have + noun	*can't stop* + verb(-ing)
I have a stomachache.	I can't stop shivering.
_____	_____
_____	_____

feel / be + adjective	noun + *hurt(s)*
I feel dizzy. / I'm dizzy.	My arm hurts.
_____	_____

Which words do you know?

scratch   rash
ear   nauseous
sneeze
high blood pressure

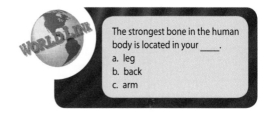

The strongest bone in the human body is located in your ____.
a. leg
b. back
c. arm

B Read the two conversations and complete the sentences. Use the correct form of *be, have, feel, can't stop,* or *hurt.*

A: What's wrong?

B: I (1) _____ exhausted. I didn't sleep well last night.

A: (2) _____ you sick? Maybe you (3) _____ a cold.

B: No, I'm fine. It's my husband, Fred—he (4) _____ the flu.

A: I'm sorry to hear that.

B: Yeah, it's pretty bad. He (5) _____ coughing. It keeps me awake at night. And now my head (6) _____.

A: Mom, my stomach (7) _____.

B: Do you (8) _____ a fever?

A: No, I don't think so.

B: Do you (9) _____ nauseous?

A: No, not at all. But you know, I did have potato chips and peanut butter for dinner.

C Use the pictures below or one of your own ideas. Tell your partner about a health problem you have. Your partner will give advice.

7 Communication   **Have you tried hypnotism?**

What do you do when you have a health problem? Who do you talk to first?

A What do you know about these different kinds of treatments?
Would you ever try any of them? Tell a partner.

 massage

 meditation

 yoga

B In groups of four, role play the following situations.

Student A: Think of a health problem. Tell your partners at least three of your symptoms.

Students B–D: Give Student A advice about the problem. Each student should recommend a different treatment: hypnotism, acupuncture, yoga, or some other treatment. You can use the notes below to help you.

Massage	Meditation
+ used to treat aches and pains	+ helps with relaxation
+ increases your flexibility	+ has been done for thousands of years
+ can help with your mood	+ can be done alone or in a group
- It can be expensive.	- It can be frustrating or boring.
Yoga	**A treatment of your choice:** _____
+ a good way to exercise	+
+ emphasizes breath control	+
+ no special equipment necessary	+
- It can be physically challenging.	-

A: I'm having trouble sleeping.

B: Well, you should try meditation.

A: Really? Have you tried it?

B: Absolutely. It really helps with relaxation.

A: I don't know . . . It sounds kind of boring . . .

C Student A chooses the treatment he or she prefers and explains why. Then switch roles and perform the role play again. Repeat until everyone has had a chance to play Student A.

Health

Lesson B   Getting better

1   Vocabulary Link   I'm sick of it!

A Read what these people said. What problem does each person have?
With a partner, take turns explaining each person's situation in your own words.

Ben

I was so excited to start college this year. Now that I'm on campus, it's been very difficult. I'm homesick—I miss my parents and friends a lot. Everything is unfamiliar here. I don't know the campus yet and I haven't made any new friends. I'm worrying so much that I'm making myself sick.

My all-time favorite band is performing on Saturday night. I haven't seen them live in four years! There's just one problem. I have class until 6:00 and then I'm scheduled to work that night. I'm thinking about cutting class and calling in sick to work so I can go to the concert. (I have a lot of sick days left, so I don't have to worry about that.)

Mary

Jill

I'm sick of my parents bossing me around[1]. I'm supposed to be at home right after school, but yesterday I came home late again. My mother said she was worried sick about me. My parents have grounded me—I can't go out with my friends for a week. They treat me like a baby even though I'm 16 years old! I can take care of myself!

[1]to boss around = to tell someone what to do

B Read these pieces of advice. Who does each one apply to?
Ben, Mary, or Jill?

1. Don't worry—you'll do well at school this year!

2. Follow the rules and try to be well-behaved.
   Your parents worry because they care about you.

3. You have a well paid job. You don't want to lose it.
   I think you should go to work.

4. You might as well listen to your parents. If you don't, they'll just get upset.

5. Get out of your room, join a club, and do something you love.

> What do these words mean?
> Which ones relate to emotions?
> Which ones are about physical feelings?
>
> airsick   carsick   homesick
> lovesick   seasick

C Look at the advice in **B**. What advice do you agree with? What advice would you offer each person?

> I think joining a club is really good advice.

> I agree. If Ben does that, he can make new friends and he won't feel so lonely.

2 Listening How's school?

A What was Ben's situation on page 75? Can you remember?
Close your book and tell a partner what you remember about Ben.

CD 2
Track 6

B Listen. What does Ben tell his mother about these things?
Write the correct letter next to items 1-3. (One item is extra.)

1. math class _____
2. roommate _____
3. the soccer team _____

A. He likes it / him.
B. He doesn't like it / him.
C. He's not sure about it / him.
D. He used to like it / him.

WORLD LINK

If you are suffering from SAD (Seasonal Affective Disorder), you feel unhappy because you don't have enough ____.
a. food
b. time
c. sunlight

CD 2
Track 6

C Listen again. Which words describe Ben? someone else?
If you checked "someone else," who is being described in each case?

	Ben	"someone else"	person described
1. an early riser	☐	☑	Ben's mother
2. homesick	☐	☐	
3. well behaved	☐	☐	
4. not feeling well	☐	☐	
5. at home after 8:00	☐	☐	

3 Reading Modern life challenges

Can modern life make you sick? Explain.

A Scan the article on page 77. What are the names of the five medical conditions mentioned?
Write the answers in the chart under "Syndrome." What do you think each one refers to?

Syndrome	Description	Possible solution
1. CHAOS	You feel embarrassed because _your house is messy_____.	
2.		
3.		
4.		
5.		

B Now read the article. Complete the chart above with the description and possible solution for each syndrome. If a solution is not mentioned, write *NM* in the chart.

1st paragraph: chaos, tidy
2nd paragraph: fatigue
3rd paragraph: straightforward
5th paragraph: gentle

C What do the words on the right mean? Work with a partner to guess the definitions. Then check your dictionary for the answers.

SURPRISING SYNDROMES OF MODERN LIFE

Margaret's friend is taking a new job in a faraway city. She wants to hold a farewell dinner party at her home. But she can't. Margaret suffers from *CHAOS (Can't Have Anyone Over Syndrome)*. Her apartment is messy and she's embarrassed by it. "I've never been a tidy person," she says. "My best friend gave me some good advice. He told me to get a maid."

These days we get and receive so much information every day. People call, text, and e-mail us all day long and they expect quick responses from us. It can be very demanding – and it's making some people sick. They have *information fatigue syndrome*. There is so much information, they become paralyzed and can't think clearly. "I can't sleep at night because I worry," says Bahman, a college senior. "I'm sick of it."

Do you sometimes engage in "deskfast" (eating breakfast at your desk at work)? If your answer is "yes," then you may suffer from hurry sickness. *Hurry sickness* is a straightforward name for another syndrome of modern life. "I'm always rushing. And I'm tired all the time. Just last week I had to call in sick because I was so stressed," says Mari, a company employee. "I'm worried about using up all of my sick days."

We've all complained about having too much work to do. Well, how about not having enough work? *Underload syndrome* is caused by having little or nothing to do at the office. Steven works as a project manager. "I can finish my work in about four hours, but I'm afraid to say anything about it. I don't want to be assigned too much work!" So what does he do? Steven pretends to be busy. "I'm thinking about getting a part-time job in the evening. That's one possible idea."

Chances are you've experienced *phone neck* before. Another name for it would be "pain in the neck," because that's what people with this condition experience. Holding the phone between your neck and your ear for a long time causes *phone neck*. How can you take care of it? Getting a gentle neck massage would be a good place to start.

ASK ANSWER

Look at where you wrote "NM" in the chart on page 76. Can you suggest some possible solutions?

Which syndrome is the worst? Why? Take a vote as a class.

4 Language Link   Reported speech: requests and commands

A   Study the chart. Can you name two differences between quoted speech and reported speech with *tell* and *ask*?

	Quoted speech	Reported speech
command	The teacher said, "<u>Begin</u> the test."	The teacher told us <u>to begin</u> the test.
	The teacher said, "<u>Don't talk</u>."	The teacher told us <u>not to talk</u>.
request	The secretary said, "Please <u>sit down</u>."	The secretary asked him <u>to sit down</u>.
	The secretary said, "Please <u>don't use</u> your cell phone."	The secretary asked him <u>not to use</u> his cell phone.

Quoted speech reports a person's exact words.
Reported speech is used to report what someone else has said (but not the exact words.)

B   Look at Tim's trip to the doctor. Complete the conversation with reported speech.

Take two tablets with meals. Get some rest. Don't overdo it.

What did the doctor say?

She _____ _____ _____ take two tablets with meals and get some rest. She also _____ _____ _____ _____ overdo it.

At the doctor's office

Later that day

C   Read the sentences in quoted speech. Then rewrite each one in reported speech. Use pronouns for the underlined words.

1. <u>Coach Jon</u> said to <u>the team</u>, "Never give up!"

   _____

2. <u>My friends</u> asked me, "Will you help <u>us</u>?"

   _____

3. <u>My sister</u> and I said to <u>our dog</u>, "Sit!"

   _____

4. <u>The librarian</u> said to <u>Mrs. Green</u>, "Please be quiet."

   _____

5. <u>Professor Lewis</u> asked <u>our class</u>, "Would you please stay after class?"

   _____

6. <u>The parents</u> said to <u>their children</u>, "Don't talk to strangers."

   _____

librarian

D   Complete these sentences with information that is true for you. Then tell a partner.

1. My parents are always telling me . . .

2. I don't like it when my friend asks me . . .

3. Our teacher often tells us . . .

4. Recently I asked my parents . . .

Professor Lewis

5 Writing   **Syndromes and solutions**

A Write about a person who has a modern-day sickness.
Include the following in your writing:

- describe the person and his or her situation
- identify the syndrome
- suggest a solution

B Exchange papers with a partner.
Suggest one more solution for
the problem.

> *My mom's friend is married*
> *and has two small children.*
> *She also works a part-time job to make*
> *extra money. She is extremely busy.*
>
> *She suffers from "hurry sickness." She*
> *is always rushing to and from work or*
> *school. I think she needs to take better*
> *care of herself. I think she should . . .*

6 Communication   **A healthy and happy life**

A Look at this list of tips for leading a healthy and happy life. Add four more tips to the list.

Tips for leading a healthy and happy life			
Get plenty of rest.	Eat healthy foods.		
Spend time with good friends.	Don't hang out with negative people.		

B Ask three different classmates: "What is important for a healthy and happy life?"
Write their names and answers in the chart.

Name	Answer
1.	
2.	
3.	

C Get into small groups. Take turns reporting
what the students you talked to said.

> Pablo told me to eat a big
> breakfast every morning.

> Tenley told me not to worry
> about my exams too much.

D Review all the advice you got in **B**. Together, choose the three best tips.

Check out the World Link video.

 Practice your English online at http://elt.heinle.com/worldlink

8 Sports and Hobbies

Lesson A In my free time

1 Vocabulary Link A great way to stay active

A Look at these statistics for marathon runners. How are the finishing times for 1980 and 2008 different? How can you explain the difference? Discuss with a partner.

B Read what Mila and Vic have to say. Then answer the questions.

- What activity are they involved in?
- In what ways are Mila and Vic different?

> Find the expressions in blue that have a similar meaning to these words:
> remain active
> participate in an activity
> leisure time activity

Average finishing time		
	1980	2008
Men	3h 32m*	4h 16m
Women	4h 3m	4h 43m

*3 hours, 32 minutes

Mila

I'm an active member of my running club. My nickname is "the flash" because I can run a marathon in three hours. I train every day. I love to run in the front—I have to be where the action is! And I used to love the New York City Marathon—but now it's not so fun because there are too many runners in the race. Many of them are not serious athletes. They just do it as a spare-time activity when they can. Some people take six, seven, or even eight hours to finish the race. I used to feel proud when I said, "I ran a marathon." Now everyone is doing it.

Vic

I retired a few years ago and had a lot of free time. I was looking for some kind of physical activity—specifically an outdoor activity—where I could improve my health. I had tried a wide range of activities: ping pong, basketball, and even swing dancing! Finally, I decided to take action. I started running by myself. It's a great way to stay active. I'm called "the penguin" because I'm so slow, but I don't mind. I may not be a professional athlete, but I love running anyway! This year, my goal is to finish in seven hours. Actually, I'll be proud if I can just finish at all!

ASK ANSWER

What do you do to stay active? For example, are you involved in any sports?

What are your favorite outdoor activities?

What things do you do in your spare time?

2 Listening   **It's time to renew it.**

A   Read the two definitions for *renew*. Then match each definition (1 or 2) with a sentence (a–d).

> 1. You can **renew** (= begin again) an activity or relationship.
>
> 2. You can also **renew** (= extend the time period of) documents.

     a. Members can <u>renew their</u> museum <u>membership</u> online.

     b. I saw him for the first time in 20 years, and we <u>renewed our friendship</u>.

     c. Where do I go to <u>renew my driver's license</u>?

     d. They <u>renewed their attacks</u> on the government.

CD 2
Track 7

B   You will hear a couple of conversations between two people. Read the items below. Then listen and select the best response to each question.

> **Conversation 1**
>
> 1. What is Andy calling Lucia about?
>   a. her gym membership
>   b. a new gym
>   c. a workout plan
>
> 2. How much is Andy offering?
>   a. 40 percent off
>   b. 20 percent off
>   c. 20 dollars off
>
> 3. What can be inferred?
>   a. Lucia exercises too much.
>   b. Lucia paid already.
>   c. Lucia hasn't met Andy before.
>
> **Conversation 2**
>
> 1. What does Deo want to do?
>   a. Drive more on the weekends.
>   b. Get rid of his car.
>   c. Take his car to work.
>
> 2. What can be inferred?
>   a. It's easy to shop in Deo's neighborhood.
>   b. Deo's car is popular.
>   c. Deo doesn't pay for parking.
>
> 3. What will Deo probably not do?
>   a. Sell his car.
>   b. Renew his license.
>   c. Get a new car.

C   Check your answers in **B** with a partner. Then explain: which definition of *renew* (1 or 2) is being used in Conversations 1 and 2?

3 Pronunciation   **Compound nouns**

CD 2
Track 8

A   In most compound nouns, the first word is strongly stressed. Listen to these examples.

     1. BOARD game   2. BASKETball   3. COMPUTER game

B   Look at the underlined nouns. Circle the stressed word in each one.

     1. Sergei is the national <u>table tennis</u> champion.   4. <u>Stamp collecting</u> can be an expensive hobby.

     2. I found a tasty recipe in my new <u>cookbook</u>.   5. I've put the best photos in my <u>photo album</u>.

     3. How many <u>comic books</u> does he have?   6. She's good at <u>baseball</u>.

C   Listen and practice saying the sentences in **B** with a partner. Be sure to stress the first word in each compound noun.

CD 2
Track 9

4 Speaking   It's played with a bat and a ball.

CD 2
Track 10

Rohan is telling Ana about cricket, a game that he likes to play. Listen to and practice the conversation with a partner. Then complete the sentences below.

Rohan: Cricket is a great game. I love it!

Ana: I've never heard of it.

Rohan: Oh, it's really popular, especially in England, India, and some other countries in Asia.

Ana: Well, how do you play?

Rohan: It's played with a bat and a ball. Oh, and you need gloves, too. You start by pitching the ball to the striker[1].

Ana: It sounds like baseball to me.

Rohan: They're similar. But in cricket, there are 11 players on a team. And you play on an oval field.

Ana: How do you win?

Rohan: The object of the game is to get more runs than the other team, and . . . hey, what time is it?

Ana: Four o'clock. Why?

Rohan: I have to go. I'm late for cricket practice!

[1]the striker = the hitter

1. Cricket is similar to _____.

2. Each team has _____ players.

3. You win when you _____.

4. You need a _____, a _____, and _____.

5 Speaking Strategy

Look at the photos and read about the game of bocce ball. With a partner, write a conversation similar to the one above. (Use the Useful Expressions.) Perform your conversation for another group.

Useful Expressions: Talking about a game	
Equipment	It's played with . . . / You don't need any special equipment.
People	There are 11 players on each team. / You are competing against each other.
Playing the game	One team starts by . . . / The game begins when . . .
How to win	The team with the most points wins. / The object is to score the most runs.
Location	It's played on a field. / It's played all over the world.

What you need:

- a small ball

- several bigger balls

- two teams of 1–4 people each

How to play:

- first throw the small ball down the field

- each team then rolls the bigger balls down the field

- score a point for the big ball that is closest to the small ball

- the team with the most points wins

6 Language Link   The present perfect vs. the present perfect continuous

A   Study the chart. How are the present perfect and present perfect continuous the same? How are they different?

Use the present perfect continuous for an action that started in the past and continues (unfinished) up to the present.		
	Present perfect continuous *have / has + been + verb (-ing)*	**Present perfect** *have / has + past participle*
continuing or finished?	I've been reading that book on marathon training. (= I'm still reading it.)	I've read that book on marathon training. (= I finished the book.)
specific number of times	NOT: ~~I've been participating in three marathons~~.	I've participated in two marathons.
with *all / for / since*	I've been living / I've lived in this house all my life. (same meaning)	

B   Tom has started a lot of activities but hasn't finished them. Look at the picture of his room. Make five sentences using verbs in the box in the present perfect continuous.

do   eat   study   talk   watch

1. _____

2. _____

3. _____

4. _____

5. _____

C   Circle the correct verb form(s) to complete each sentence. (In some cases, both answers are possible.)

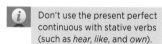
Don't use the present perfect continuous with stative verbs (such as *hear*, *like*, and *own*).

1. My mom has been working / has worked there since 1992.

2. He's been marrying / been married three times.

3. I have always been loving / have always loved a wide range of activities.

4. She's been looking / looked for a new job recently.

5. We've been studying / studied for four hours already. Let's take a break!

6. I've just been finishing / finished my final exams. They were hard!

7. Have you been hearing / heard the good news? We won the championship!

D   Write answers that are true for you. Then share your answers with a partner.

Name something you've been doing a lot recently: _____

Name someone who has been living in the same place for more than 10 years: _____

Name something you've been studying for a long time that you don't like: _____

7 Communication   Who is telling the truth?

A Write about two things you started in the past and still do today.

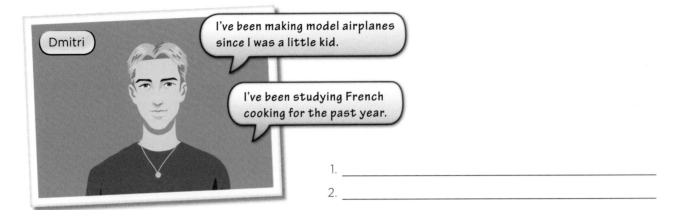

Dmitri

I've been making model airplanes since I was a little kid.

I've been studying French cooking for the past year.

1. _____
2. _____

B In a group of three, follow these instructions.

1. Look at the six sentences your group wrote in **A**. Choose one to talk about.

2. Ask the student who wrote the sentence as many questions as possible about the sentence. You will have two minutes to learn everything you can.

C Read the instructions. Then take turns playing the game as a class.

1. Now the group of three students stands in front of the class. All three students say the sentence they chose in **B**. Two students lie, but they want the class to believe that they are the ones who have had the experience.

I've been studying French cooking for the past year.

Dmitri   Carmen   Kumiko

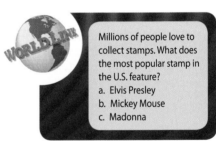

Millions of people love to collect stamps. What does the most popular stamp in the U.S. feature?
a. Elvis Presley
b. Mickey Mouse
c. Madonna

2. The other students in the class ask the members of the group questions. They have two minutes to find out which student is telling the truth, and which two are lying.

Carmen, what's one dish you've learned to make?

Dmitri, what's one dish you've learned to make?

Kumiko, where exactly have you been studying?

Sports and Hobbies

Lesson B   The active life

1   Vocabulary Link   **Around the world by car**

A   Read this interview with Guy Denis. Study the words in blue.
Which ones do you know already? Then answer the questions.

1. What is Guy preparing for?   2. Why is he doing it?   3. How does he feel about it?

Guy Denis is going to head out on a wild adventure: a trip around the world by car! Read all about his plans in our exclusive interview!

You're traveling around the world by car. How does that work exactly?
Obviously I can't drive across the ocean! When I can't drive, I'll ship the car by boat and then fly to the next place to get it.

How are you preparing for this trip?
I'm buying a car, a portable shower, and a tent. I also have to spend some extra money on a special stove that runs on unleaded gasoline. I spent everything paying for this stuff!

What are you most worried about?
Every day I'm going to wake up by myself. I'll definitely miss my wife and little boy, of course.

Isn't it dangerous?
I've been warned about some places. I plan to travel with an escort in those areas. I'm not afraid to ask for help when I need it.

What about the food? And the weather?
I'm going to have to deal with a lot of changes, that's for sure.

What are you looking forward to?
It's going to be interesting to stay in all these different places. I happen to be from Paris originally, so I'll be there a few extra days. It will be nice to stay with my parents and get a nice, home cooked meal.

Why are you doing this now?
Because I'm old enough to do it responsibly but young enough to really enjoy it. I want to know all about the world. This journey has been a dream of mine for a long time—and I believe in following your dreams.

Any last thoughts?
I want to thank my friends and family for all their support. I couldn't do this without their help!

B   Imagine you are traveling around the world by car with a friend for one year.
Plan your trip. Answer each question with a single sentence.

- How would you prepare for the trip? Who would you ask for help?
- Who would you like to travel with? Which cities would you stay in?
- During your travels, what would you spend the most money on?
- What would be the hardest thing to deal with?

C   Share your answers with a partner.

2 Listening   Choose the best response.

CD 2
Track 11

Listen to each question or statement and three possible responses. Circle the best response (A, B, or C).

1. A   B   C   5. A   B   C

2. A   B   C   6. A   B   C

3. A   B   C   7. A   B   C

4. A   B   C   8. A   B   C

3 Reading   A star in the X Games

A   Look at the title of the reading and the photos on page 87.
Ask and answer these questions with a partner.

- Have you ever heard of the X Games?

- Can you name any sports that are played at these games?

B   Now scan the article. Add at least two examples to each item in the chart below.

Item	Examples
1. locations of the X Games	Barcelona
2. summer sports	
3. categories of in-line skating	
4. winter sports	
5. regional teams in the global championships	

C   Read these statements about Fabiola. Then find a sentence in the reading that supports each statement.

1. Fabiola's mom didn't make a lot of money. _____

2. There are not many female athletes. _____

3. Fabiola wins against women. _____

4. Fabiola wins against men. _____

5. Fabiola isn't married. _____

6. Fabiola is well-known outside her own country. _____

7. Fabiola is South American. _____

8. Fabiola has her own sense of style. _____

All About the X Games

The first Extreme Games competition was held in 1995 in Rhode Island, USA. The athletes competed in nine events, including windsurfing and mountain biking.

The Extreme Games were renamed and became the X Games.

The first Winter X Games were held in California, USA. The athletes competed in events such as snowboarding and ice climbing.

The first Asian X Games were held in Phuket, Thailand.

The first European X Games were held in Barcelona, Spain.

The first Latin American X Games were held in Rio de Janeiro, Brazil.

A Star in the X Games

There's a new kind of competition happening worldwide. No, it's not the World Cup. It's the X Games.

In different areas of the world, athletes train and compete in their own versions of the X Games. The best athletes can advance to the global championship. At the championship, teams from six regions (Asia, Australia, Canada, Europe, South America, and the United States) face each other. There are summer sports (in-line skating, biking, and skateboarding) and winter ones (skiing and snowboarding). Most "X Gamers" are male, but there are a few women. One woman, Fabiola da Silva stands out from the crowd. She's an in-line skater, she comes from Brazil, and she's easily recognizable with her tank top and nose ring.

There are two different in-line skating categories: park and vert. In the park event, skaters compete on a course that has ledges, handrails, and other obstacles. In the vert event, skaters do tricks on a half pipe. They try to fly high in the air and spin. Fabiola competes in both events and has won six gold medals in the vert event, her specialty. She has been skating for years and has dominated the women's events.

skating on a half pipe

Fabiola would like to see more women in the X Games, but she's not afraid of the guys. Ever since she received her first pair of skates at the age of 12, she's played with boys. Now she skates in competitions with them and she beats many of them.

Fabiola's mother was a housekeeper and life was hard, but she saved her money to buy Fabiola's skates. It was a good investment. Fabiola has traveled abroad for events and has become famous in the international skating world.

Success hasn't gone to her head, though. She's a typical young woman of the world: she has a boyfriend, likes to listen to rock music, and prefers healthy foods. And she doesn't seem to care much about the attention she gets.

ASK ANSWER

Who are some popular female athletes you know? What sports do they play?

Which would you rather see, the Olympics or the X Games? Why?

4 Language Link   The simple past tense vs. the perfect tenses

A Study the chart and do the following:

- Complete sentences a and b with the correct form of the verb *visit*.

- Complete sentences c and d with the correct form of the verb *study*.

	Completed past actions	Past actions continuing up to now
Simple past	a. I _____ Santiago, Chile last year.[1]	
Present perfect	b. I _____ Santiago twice.[2]	c. I _____ English since April.[3]
Present perfect continuous		d. I _____ English for one year.[3]

[1]Notice the specific time expression "last year."
[2]It happened at an indefinite time in the past.
[3]Note that both *for* and *since* can be used with these tenses.

B Read about mountain climber Erik Weihenmayer. Complete the sentences with the verbs in parentheses. Use the present perfect or the present perfect continuous.

Erik Weihenmayer (1. be) _____ blind since he was 13.
He (2. climb) _____ since he was 16 and he isn't finished yet.

He (3. climb) _____ Mount Everest already. In fact, he
(4. reach) _____ the top of the Seven Summits—the seven
tallest mountains on seven continents.

He (5. develop) _____ his own climbing system. His partners
wear bells on their vests. He follows the sounds of the bells.

Erik is not sure about his next plan. He (6. think) _____ about
it for a long time.

C Circle the correct verb form to complete each sentence. For one
item, both answers are possible.

I learned / I've learned how to play dominoes from my
grandfather many years ago. He taught / He's been teaching
me the game during my summer break from school.

My cousin is 20 years old. He played / He's been playing
dominoes since he was seven years old. He's gone / He's been going
to dominoes competitions. Last year he got / he's gotten second
place in a really big contest. He's always done / He's always been
doing well under pressure. I think he'll win first prize this year.

My grandfather has played / has been playing the game for 50
years. He says he's played / he's been playing about 20,000 games
and has no plans to stop. He loves it too much!

D Compare your answers in **B** and **C** with a partner.
Explain your choices.

> What did you choose for
> number one in Exercise B?

> I chose the present
> perfect because . . .

5 Writing   Go, team, go!

A Write about an experience you had playing for, watching, training with, or cheering for a club or team.

B Exchange papers with a partner. Ask your partner a question about the experience he or she described.

THE KARATE CLUB
I want to tell you about my experience training with the karate club. It was physically very difficult. Every day after school we met outside the gym. First we would stretch. Then we would go for a one-mile run to warm up. After that . . .

6 Communication   I'm known for . . .

A With a partner, complete the chart with the names of famous people whom you know something about.

Actor	
Singer	
Athlete	
Other (your idea)	

B Choose one of the famous people in **A**. Complete the sentences about him or her. Then write the questions you would ask to get that information.

Sentences	Questions
1. I was born in _____ .	When / Where were you born?
2. I became famous because _____ .	
3. I've been _____ for / since _____ .	
4. I got interested in _____ when I _____ .	
5. I'm popular in _____ .	
6. I've recently been in the news because _____ .	

C Join another pair. Use the questions in **B** to interview the other pair. Can you guess their famous person's name?

> How long have you been playing baseball professionally?

> I've been playing for more than five years now.

 Check out the World Link video.   Practice your English online at http://elt.heinle.com/worldlink

1   Vocabulary Link   Are you old enough to vote?

A   Doris Chavez and Amelia Smith are running for mayor. Read their ads.
Then answer the questions by checking the correct box(es) with a partner.

DORIS CHAVEZ for mayor!

*"We're making progress in many areas . . .
why change now? Reelect Doris Chavez!"*

In her first **term**, Mayor Chavez
- **launched** a new school lunch program for elementary school students
- **taxed** large companies to raise extra money
- has worked **enthusiastically** to improve life for everyone—crime is down 30%

*There is no better **candidate** than Doris Chavez for mayor!*

AMELIA SMITH for mayor! ★ ★ ★ ★ ★ ★

*"No more politics **as usual**. It's time for change in our city! Elect Amelia Smith!"*

Amelia Smith **vows**
- to **expand** the school lunch program to include older students
- not to raise taxes on **corporations** or individuals
- to work hard for all **citizens** to keep our city streets safe

★ ★

Amelia Smith is the clear choice for mayor!

	Doris	Amelia
1. Who is currently the mayor?	☐	☐
2. Who doesn't want to increase taxes?	☐	☐
3. Who is interested in the school lunch program?	☐	☐
4. Who mentions crime and safety?	☐	☐

B   Look at the information in **A**. Find the word(s) in blue to complete these definitions.

1. doing (something) the same way ___as usual___

2. eagerly, with great energy _____

3. a fixed period of time _____

4. increase in size _____

5. large companies _____

6. started _____

7. promises _____

8. moving forward _____

9. obvious _____

10. a person who is competing for a position _____

11. members of a city or country _____

12. made someone pay money to the government _____

> **ⓘ** The prefix *re-* can mean "to do again." In which of these words does *re-* have that meaning?
>
> rebuild   remarry   return
> reelect   research   rewrite

ASK ANSWER

What is the voting age where you live? Are you old enough to vote? too young to vote?

Think of a person who was up for reelection recently. Did people vote for or vote against him or her? Why?

2 Listening   **Together we can do it.**

A   Read the sentences below. What does the word in blue mean? When do election campaigns typically happen?

There are two candidates running for mayor. The election campaign will run from February 1 to March 15.

CD 2
Track 12

B   Listen to the beginning of speeches given by Doris and Amelia. Choose the best answer to complete each sentence. (There is one extra.)

1. Doris is giving her speech because
2. Amelia is giving her speech because

a. she is going to run for mayor.
b. she has been elected mayor.
c. she has lost the race for mayor.

CD 2
Track 12

C   Listen again. Choose the best answers.

1. When Doris says *never in my wildest dreams* she means . . .
   a. she was pretty sure.
   b. she couldn't imagine it.

2. When Doris says *I gave it my best shot* she means . . .
   a. she was very disappointed.
   b. she worked really hard.

3. When Amelia says *Doris and I were running neck and neck* she means . . .
   a. they had almost the same number of votes.
   b. there was a clear winner.

4. When Amelia says *we saw a record turnout* she means . . .
   a. a large number of people voted.
   b. a small number of people voted.

CD 2
Track 13

D   Now listen to the rest of Amelia's speech. Check the topics she refers to in her speech. What key words in the listening helped you choose your answers? Tell a partner.

☐ the economy   ☐ public transportation   ☐ crime   ☐ pollution   ☐ education

> **ASK ANSWER**
> Look at the topics in **D**.
> Which one do you think is the biggest problem where you live? Why?

3 Pronunciation   **Sentence level stress**

A   Read these sentences from Amelia's speech aloud. Underline the stressed (content) words.

1. We need to rebuild downtown.
2. We need to make our streets safer.
3. We should build more schools.
4. Let's prepare our children for the future.
5. Together we can do it!

CD 2
Track 14

B   Listen and check your answers.

> Remember! **Content** (information) **words** are often stressed. **Function words** are usually unstressed.
>
> Content words include: nouns, main verbs, adjectives, adverbs, *this/that*, question words
>
> Function words include: *a/an/the, but/so/or,* auxiliary verbs, personal pronouns

4 Speaking I'd like to talk to you about . . .

CD 2
Track 15

A Listen to the brief speech below. What is the problem? What is one thing causing it? Can you think of other causes?

> Today I'd like to talk to you about rush hour traffic. I'll begin by telling you about the problem. Then I'll list the three things I think are causing this problem.
>
> So, let's start by talking about rush hour traffic in this city. We've all experienced it, and in recent years it's gotten worse. Ten years ago, it used to take about 45 minutes to drive across town. Now it takes two hours. One of the main causes of this problem is too many cars on the road. More cars means more traffic and, of course, more traffic accidents. Another cause of rush hour traffic is . . .

5 Speaking Strategy

A Match each word on the left with one on the right to make a list of common city problems. Can you add to the list?

unaffordable	high	streets	unemployment
dirty	noise	housing	pollution

B Choose one of the community problems in **A** or one of your own. Work with a partner and complete the information below.

Problem:

_____

Causes of the problem:

1. _____

2. _____

3. _____

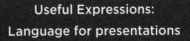

> **Useful Expressions:**
> **Language for presentations**
>
> **Stating the purpose**
>
> Today, I'd like to talk to you about . . .
>
> I'll begin by (talking about the issue). / I'll provide an overview of (the issue).
>
> Then I'll list the (two / three / four) . . .
>
> **Stating important points**
>
> Let's talk first about . . .
>
> One of the main causes (of rush hour traffic) is . . .
>
> Another / A second cause of . . . is . . .
>
> And finally . . .

C Join another pair and follow the instructions.

Presenters: Use the language for presentations to explain your problem in **B** clearly. One person should introduce the talk. The second person should explain the causes of the problem.

Listeners: Take notes. After the presentation, give suggestions for how to solve the problem.

6 Language Link *Too* and *enough*

A Study the chart. Notice the uses of *too* and *enough*.

Too + adjective and *too much / too many* + noun indicate "more than is necessary."	
It's too dark. Can you turn on the light please?	It's crowded. There's too much traffic. It's crowded. There are too many people here.
Adjective + *enough* and *enough* + noun mean "sufficient(ly)."	
It's bright enough. We don't need that lamp. It isn't bright enough. We need more light.	There's enough room for one more person. There are enough people here. Let's begin.

B Write *too*, *too much*, or *too many* next to each noun.

1. _____ citizens   4. _____ taxes   7. _____ crime

2. _____ dangerous   5. _____ information 8. _____ votes

3. _____ furniture   6. _____ enthusiastic 9. _____ pollution

C Correct the errors with *too* or *enough* below. Check your answers with a partner.

1. I can't button this shirt. It isn't too big.

2. It's not dangerous here. It's enough safe to go out at night by yourself.

3. It's crowded. There are too much people in this little room.

4. These condos are expensive enough to buy. We need more affordable housing.

5. He's only 12 years old. He's old enough to drive.

D Write down your complaints about the items in the box.
Use *too much*, *too many*, or *not enough*.

affordable housing	job opportunities	police officers
crime	noise pollution	traffic jams

1. _____

2. _____

3. _____

4. _____

5. _____

6. _____

> There isn't enough affordable housing in our city.

> I know. It's expensive to buy an apartment here.

E Discuss the complaints from **D** with a partner.

7 Communication   Did you sleep enough last night?

A   Follow the instructions to complete the survey below.

- **For questions 1-6:** Write *enough* before or after each word. (Only one position is correct.)

- **For questions 7-12:** Write *too*, *too much*, or *too many*.

	Yes	No
1. Did you _____ sleep _____ last night?	☐	☐
2. Do you have _____ credits _____ to graduate?	☐	☐
3. Is it _____ quiet _____ for you to study at home?	☐	☐
4. Do you typically have _____ time _____ to finish your homework?	☐	☐
5. Have you had _____ to eat _____ today?	☐	☐
6. Do you get along _____ well _____ with your parents?	☐	☐

	Yes	No
7. Do you spend _____ time watching TV?	☐	☐
8. Is English _____ difficult to learn?	☐	☐
9. Do you sometimes eat _____ sweets?	☐	☐
10. Do you have _____ problems in your life?	☐	☐
11. Is it possible to earn _____ money?	☐	☐
12. At 20, are people _____ young to get married?	☐	☐

B   Use the questions in **A** to interview a partner. Ask follow-up questions.

> Is it quiet enough for you to study at home?

> No, not really. It's pretty noisy.

> Where do you study then?

> I do most of my studying at the library.

Social Issues

Lesson B People, people, everywhere!

1 Vocabulary Link   The problem of sprawl

> **spread** + adverb: *spread quickly*
>
> **spread** + noun: *spread a rumor, spread the news, spread jam (on toast)*

A Look at the photo and read the definition of the word *sprawl*. Do you know any places where sprawl is a problem?

> **sprawl** = (n.) ugly, unplanned growth of a city into the countryside

B Read Jared's essay about his hometown. Notice the words in blue. Circle the ones you already know.

Sprawl is a problem in my city. In the past five years, there has been a lot of new development, especially homes. As development spreads across the land, it destroys parks, farms, and other open spaces.

In my neighborhood, we live far away from public transportation, stores, and schools. That forces us to drive longer distances. More driving means more pollution. This reliance on our cars is a problem. Ambulances have to travel farther to hospitals. It's a waste of our tax money.

I support a law that provides money for new walking and bicycling paths in my neighborhood to encourage people to leave their cars at home for short trips. I also think we need to protect our open spaces so that future generations have beautiful places to relax. Finally, I think we can improve the air quality by carpooling more with our friends and neighbors.

C Write the missing blue word from **B** to complete each definition.

1. ___encourage___ : to persuade or get someone to do something
2. _____ : to damage completely
3. _____ : to keep something safe
4. _____ : to move gradually outward
5. _____ : to use badly
6. _____ : to offer or give something
7. _____ : to make someone do something difficult

Verb	Noun
	destruction
develop	
	encouragement
	force
	improvement
	protection
rely	
	support
	waste

D Complete the chart on the right with blue words in **B**. Look up any words you don't know.

E Work with a partner. Without looking back at **B**, try to answer these questions in your own words.

1. What happens when people live far away from public transportation, stores, and schools?
2. What does Jared support? What does Jared want to encourage people to do? What does he want to protect? Why?

2 Listening Urban or suburban?

A Do you prefer to live in an urban or suburban area? Why? Explain your reasons to a partner.

urban

suburban

CD 2
Track 16

B Listen to each person talk about urban and suburban life. Follow the directions.

1. Match each speaker to her photo. Write A, B, or C in the photo.

2. Where do they live now? Where do they want to live in the future? Write "U" for urban and "S" for suburban. Write "NM" if the information is "not mentioned."

A. Bella

B. Anne

C. Mercedes

now: _____
future: _____

now: _____
future: _____

now: _____
future: _____

CD 2
Track 17

C Read the three sentences. What do you think the underlined expressions mean? Which person from **B** do you think would probably say each sentence? Listen and write the names.

1. I hope I can move—I have to <u>wait and see</u>, I guess.   _____

2. Now that I've <u>put down roots</u>, I probably won't move.   _____

3. I needed <u>a change of scenery</u> and I got it!   _____

3 Reading Shrinking population

ⓘ shrink = to get smaller

A Look at the title on page 97. What is the reading mainly about?

a. the world's overpopulation problem

b. the decreasing birthrate in some places

c. the role of family in two countries

B These numbers are missing from the first paragraph of the reading.
Can you write them in? Guess with a partner.

6   12   111   1960   3,500

THE SHRINKING FAMILY
In some countries, has population control gone too far?

Did you know that

- It took only [   ] years—from 1987 to 1999—for the population of the world to increase by one *billion* people. The world's population now stands at over [   ] *billion* people.
- There were [   ] cities with more than one million people in [   ]. By 1995 there were 280.
- Every 20 minutes, [   ] new lives are added to the world's population.

In many countries, the population continues to grow and create a lot of new problems. Interestingly, however, family size is not increasing everywhere in the world. As men and women get married later in life and have more economic worries, they are being forced to make difficult decisions. As a result, some women are having fewer babies.

Experts believe that the education of women is important for successful population control. When women and young girls are educated, they participate more in family decisions: They have a voice in improving their own lives.

In both Mexico and Italy, family planning programs and new job opportunities for women have changed everything.

Elisa Sanchez is a mother in Monterrey, Mexico. She and her husband are both high school teachers in their thirties. They have two children. They don't plan to have any more. "I was one of six children," says Elisa, "My husband comes from a family of seven. People used to have more children and those children supported their parents in old age. But now it's different."

Elisa's husband thinks the lower birthrate is a positive change. "With a smaller population, there will be less competition. That means there will be more job opportunities for young people."

Gina Moretti works hard as a TV news announcer in Milan, Italy. "My mother thinks I work too hard. Every time I visit her she asks me the same question: When are you getting married? She thinks I need a man to rely on. But actually, I can provide for myself just fine. I'm very independent."

Gina is 32 and her mother is worried about Gina's ability to get married and raise a family in the future. The Italian government is worried, too. In 1958, one million babies were born in Italy. In 1998, it was half that number. The average mother in Italy has her first child at the age of 30. After 30, experts note, there isn't a lot of time for women to have many children. The population is aging rapidly and there are fewer young people to support these seniors. Some wonder: has population control in Italy been *too* successful?

C Read the article. Complete the sentences with correct information.

1. Couples are having fewer children because _____.

2. Experts want to educate women and young girls because then they will be able to

_____.

3. In the past, people had big families so that the children would _____.

4. One of the "pros" of a lower birthrate is _____.

5. One of the "cons" of a lower birthrate is _____.

ASK ANSWER

Can you think of one more advantage of having a lower birthrate? What's one more disadvantage?

4 Language Link   **Future real conditionals**

A Study the chart. Circle the correct answer to complete each sentence.

If clause	Result clause
If it rains,	I'm going to cancel the picnic.
If we don't win the game,	we'll be eliminated.

> *i* You can also put the result clause first with no change in meaning:
>
> *I'm going to cancel the picnic if it rains.*

1. Future real conditionals describe future situations that are possible / impossible.

2. The verb in the *if* clause is in the simple present / future.

3. In the result clause, a present / future form is used.

B Look at the verbs in the box. Use the simple present or future tense to complete the sentences. (You will use one verb twice.)

be	~~get~~	invite	make	not pass	not say	not study
educate	have	leave	miss	~~save~~	see	

1. You ___*'ll save*___ money if you ___*get*___ a roommate.

2. If I _____ all weekend, I _____ the test on Monday.

3. I _____ hello if I _____ him on the street.

4. If I _____ a party, I _____ you.

5. If you _____ early, you _____ all the fun.

6. It _____ better for the Earth if couples _____ smaller families.

7. If we _____ women, they _____ better decisions.

C Answer each question with two future real conditional sentences. Then ask and answer the questions with a partner.

What will happen if . . .

1. there's no more oil?

   If there's no more oil, people will have to find alternative energy supplies.

   _____

2. the world's population continues to increase?

   _____

   _____

3. the Earth's temperature gets warmer and warmer?

   _____

   _____

5 Writing   **What will happen if . . . ?**

A Look back at page 98, Exercise **C**. Write an explanation of your response to one of the questions. Describe both the positive and negative effects.

B Exchange papers with a partner. Tell your partner one thing you learned from reading his or her paper.

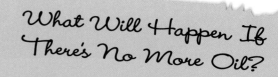

What Will Happen If There's No More Oil?

If there's no more oil, there will be a lot of problems. Corporations need oil for energy. We need it for transportation and to heat our homes. I think the world economy will . . .

It's not all bad, however. Without oil, we will have to develop . . .

6 Communication   **You're in charge!**

A Read each problem. Work with a partner and suggest answers for each problem.

Problem: Our schools don't have enough money for new technology.

Suggestions:

1. Raise taxes to pay for better computers.
2. Ask people to donate

Problem: Young people are leaving rural areas and moving to big cities.

Suggestions:

1. Give people money to encourage them to stay in their hometowns.
2. Ask corporations to provide

Problem: New development is getting out of control in the suburbs.

Suggestions:

1. Limit the number of new homes being built each month.
2. Support a law to

B Imagine you are running for political office. Prepare a short speech. Include suggestions to the problems in **A** in your speech.

C Present your speech to a partner.
What does your partner think of your ideas?

> Our schools don't have enough money for new technology. The classrooms need new computers and better technology. If I get elected, I'll raise taxes . . .

Check out the World Link video.

Practice your English online at http://elt.heinle.com/worldlink

1 Storyboard

A Mr. Stevens and his son, Ian, are waiting in the doctor's office. Look at the pictures and complete the conversations. More than one answer is possible for each blank.

B Practice the conversation in groups of four. Then change roles and practice again.

C With a partner, create and perform your own conversation between a doctor and a patient.

2 See It and Say It

A Look at the picture. Use the words in the box to talk about it. Then answer the questions with a partner.

> campaign   citizens   speech
> candidate   election   term
>   running for (a political office)

- Is this Mr. Gold's first political campaign?

- Look at the banner. Which of these ideas does Mr. Gold support?
  building more schools   encouraging public transportation
  raising taxes   stopping business development

- Who do you think will vote for Mike Gold? Who is going to vote against him?

B Work with a partner. Write a brief speech for Mike Gold. Perform your speech for another pair.

3 I'm Exhausted Because . . .

A Match Camille's behaviors on the left with the causes on the right. Compare your answers with a partner.

1. Camille is scratching her leg.
2. She's dizzy and hungry.
3. She's breathing hard.
4. She's shivering.
5. She's just swallowed two aspirin.

a. She's been playing tennis for two hours.
b. She forgot to bring her coat.
c. She was bitten by a mosquito.
d. She skipped breakfast and lunch.
e. She has a headache.

B In 2-3 minutes, add as many items as you can to each category.

Things that make you . . .

1. cough: _____ *cigarette smoke,* _____

2. feel exhausted: _____

3. feel dizzy: _____

4. shiver: _____

C Ask a partner questions beginning with *What makes you . . . ?* for each category above.

4 Terry's Diary

A Use the words in the box to complete Terry's diary entry about living in the city. (Three words are extra.)

action	jams
active	noise
activity	opportunities
affordable	taxes
dirty	transportation
in	with

Last night I went out with some old friends. They're all married and live in the suburbs. I'm single and still live in the city. They wanted to know why I still live here.

It's true—living in the city can be annoying sometimes. We have a problem with _____ streets. Plus, there's a lack of _____ housing. Everything is so expensive! The _____ pollution is pretty bad, too. You have to deal _____ a lot of hassles every day.

On the other hand, the city is pretty great! First of all, there are a lot of job _____ here. I certainly have a well-paying job! The traffic _____ can be pretty bad, but I avoid them. I take public _____ everywhere. I also stay _____ by walking all over the city.

The city is where all the _____ is and I love it here!

B What kind of hassles (difficult or frustrating situations) do you have to deal with in your city? Make a list with a partner.

5 Poker Tips

A Read these pieces of information given by a professional about how to play poker well. Rewrite each tip in reported speech, using the verb in parentheses.

1. Learn the different kinds of cards. (tell)

   _____

2. Don't bet too much money. (ask)

   _____

3. Study the other players' facial expressions. (ask)

   _____

4. Don't take unnecessary risks. (tell)

   _____

B Now think of a sport or game that you know how to play. Complete the sentences below. Don't show anyone!

People: There are . . . people on each team. / You play by yourself.

Equipment: The game is played with . . .

Location: It's played in / on . . .

Playing the game: The game starts when . . .

How to win: The object of the game is . . .

C With a partner, take turns asking and answering questions about each other's sport or game. Can you guess what it is?

> Is it a sport?

> No. It's a card game.

> How many people play it?

> Four to six people play it. There aren't any teams— you play by yourself.

6 Listening

**CD 2
Track 18**

You are going to hear a lecture. Complete the notes. Write no more than two words for each answer. Then answer the question below.

In which class would you probably hear this lecture?

☐ science

☐ math

☐ business

I. Dehydration: defined

A. Most of your body's weight is due to _____ —about _____%.

B. Dehydration occurs when the amount of water _____ the body is greater than the amount _____.

   1. "I'm dehydrated" means _____.

II. Causes

A. You can become dehydrated when you _____ a lot or are _____ on a hot day.

III. Symptoms

A. Include a _____ and getting _____.

   1. If you remain dehydrated, you may have to go to _____.

1   Vocabulary Link   Money quiz

A   Answer the questions about money below.

Money Quiz

1. What are two fun things you like to do when you're broke (= don't have any money)?

2. What is one thing you can't afford to buy right now, but really want?

3. What jobs do you think pay way too much? Which ones pay next to nothing?

4. My budget: I can get by (= survive) on _____ a week.

5. What do you do when you are short on money (= don't have enough)?

6. How much money do you owe on credit cards?

7. Which statement do you agree with?

   ☐ It's OK to borrow a large amount of money as long as you pay it back. (= return the money)

   ☐ You should never borrow money and go into debt (= owe money). It's always a bad idea.

8. You are getting money out of the ATM. Can you put these steps in order?

   ☐ Enter your PIN (personal identification number).

   ☐ Insert (= put inside) your bank card into the machine.

   ☐ Select (= choose) the amount of money you want.

   ☐ Take the money and receipt and walk away.

   ☐ The machine will return your card. Put it away (in your pocket or purse).

B   Ask and answer questions 1-7 from **A** with a partner. Record your partner's answers below.

1. _____

2. _____

3. _____

4. _____

5. _____

6. _____

7. _____

> So, what are two fun things you like to do when you're broke?

> I like to hang out with my friends and go window shopping. I can't afford to buy anything expensive, but it's still fun to look!

2 Listening   **Rich and poor**

CD 2
Track 19

A Listen to four short conversations. What are the people talking about? Write the number of the conversation next to the picture.

CD 2
Track 19

B Listen again. Which statement is probably true? Circle one sentence for each conversation.

1. a. Laura had just been to the supermarket.

   b. The police will find the car.

2. a. Salary is important to the man.

   b. The man doesn't need the job.

3. a. The man has never tried the powder.

   b. The woman is trying to take care of herself.

4. a. The man has been to St. James before.

   b. It's wintertime now.

CD 2
Track 20

C Listen to part of each conversation. How are the words *rich* and *poor* used? Fill in the missing words. Then match *rich* or *poor* to its definition.

1. "Poor _____!"

2. a poor _____

3. rich in _____

4. a rich _____

a. below average

b. full of

c. an expression used to show sympathy

d. interesting and colorful

3 Pronunciation   **Linking the same consonant sound**

CD 2
Track 21

A Mr. Rich is a millionaire. Listen to what he says about his children (Stan, Will, and Taylor) and his dog (Sam). Listen to how the linked sounds are pronounced.

1. "My kids still ask me for money!"

2. "Stan never visits me. I feel lonely."

3. "Will loves money. He spends so much of it!"

4. "Taylor really has too much fun. She doesn't take anything seriously."

5. "I love Sam most of all. He's a good dog."

B Practice saying the sentences in **A** to your partner. Be sure to pronounce the linked sounds only once.

4 Speaking — Where's my soda?

CD 2
Track 22

A Mike got takeout from a nearby restaurant. Listen to the conversation. Underline the two apologies. How do Eva and Mike respond to the apologies? Circle them.

Eva: Thanks for picking up lunch, Mike.

Mike: Sure.

Eva: How much do I owe you?

Mike: Your total comes to $10.20. You can just give me ten dollars.

Eva: OK. Oh, wait . . . Sorry, I've only got a twenty-dollar bill. I wish I had something smaller . . .

Mike: Don't worry about it. Why don't we eat first and then you can pay me later?

Eva: Oh, OK. Thanks.

Mike: No problem . . . OK, here you go: A hamburger and fries for me—and a turkey sandwich for you.

Eva: Um, where's my soda?

Mike: Oh, no! I forgot your soda. Sorry . . . my mistake.

Eva: No problem. It happens. I'll just have water instead.

B Practice the conversation with a partner.

5 Speaking Strategy

A Look at each situation. What happened in each one?

B Imagine that you are one of the people in **A**. With a partner, use the Useful Expressions to apologize and accept the apology. Then choose the other situation and switch roles.

Useful Expressions: Apologizing		Useful Expressions: Accepting an apology
small accident or mistake	**serious accident or mistake**	Don't worry about it.
I'm sorry. It was an accident.	I'm really sorry that I forgot to . . .	Oh, that's OK.
Sorry. My mistake.	I'm so sorry about damaging . . .	No problem. It happens.
I can't believe I did that.	I want to apologize for what happened.	Apology accepted.

6 Language Link   *Wish*-statements

A Study the chart about *wish*-statements.

To express impossible or unlikely wishes about present situations, use a *wish* statement. The verb following *wish* is in the past.				
Present situation				***Wish*-statement**
My car **won't** start.	will	→	would	I **wish** (that) my car **would** start.
I can't **speak** Russian.	can	→	could	I **wish** (that) I **could** speak Russian.
I **am** not tall.	am	→	were*	I **wish** (that) I **were** tall.
She **doesn't have** a car.	have	→	had	She **wishes** (that) she **had** a car.
* *Were* is considered more correct than *was* in *wish*-statements.				

B Read each sentence. Then write a *wish*-statement.

1. I'm not famous.

_____

2. I'm broke.

_____

3. She has to work hard.

_____

4. He won't pay me back.

_____

5. I can't afford designer clothes.

_____

6. They've gone into debt.

_____

C Read this joke about Dumb Dave. Complete the sentences with *wish . . . could* and the verb in parentheses. Why is the character called Dumb Dave?

One day, a genie appeared to Dumb Dave and his three friends. The genie said, "I will give each of you one wish. Don't waste it!"

The first friend said, "(1. fly) _____." Her wish was granted and she flew away. The second friend said, "(2. live) _____ in a big mansion."
He suddenly disappeared too. The third friend said, "(3. be) _____ a famous actor starring in my own movie." She, too, disappeared.

Dumb Dave looked around and saw that he was alone. Then he said, "I'm lonely. Where have my three friends gone? (4. have) _____ them back here with me now . . ."

a genie

D Imagine that a genie has given you three wishes. What will you wish for? On a separate piece of paper, write three *wish*-statements and share them with a partner.

7 Communication   My wish list

A Philip is bored. He is daydreaming about his wish list. What can you say about him based on his list? Tell a partner.

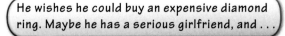
He wishes he could buy an expensive diamond ring. Maybe he has a serious girlfriend, and . . .

My Wish List
1. buy a diamond ring
2. run my own company
3. take a long vacation
4. play in the World Cup
5. buy a house in the suburbs
6. star in a big budget movie

B What things do you want to change in your life? Write a wish list for yourself. Use three of these topics.

- ☐ time
- ☐ money
- ☐ home
- ☐ fun
- ☐ vacation
- ☐ friends
- ☐ appearance
- ☐ other:_____

C Exchange wish lists with a partner.
What does your list tell you about him or her?
Ask questions about each wish.

Your list says you wish that you were taller. Why?

I love basketball. If I were taller, no one could stop me!

WORLDLINK
The Make a Wish Foundation helps sick children realize their dreams. To date, they have granted more than ____ wishes.
a. 8,500
b. 85,000
c. 185,000

Having It All

Lesson B   Striking it rich

1   Vocabulary Link   You're a winner!

A   Imagine you've won a huge amount of money in a lottery. Discuss these questions with a partner.

- What would you do first?
- Who would you tell?
- Would you prefer to receive the money in one payment or over a period of years?
- What would you do with the money?

B   Jack Wilson won millions of dollars in the lottery. Think about your answers in **A** and read Jack's story below. Then discuss the questions with a partner.

- How was Jack's behavior different from what you would do?
- Are you surprised by Jack's story?

Jack Wilson worked as an elevator repairman. One day in March, he struck it rich—he won the lottery. For Jack, who had never won anything before, the prize money was a shock. It was easy money—he didn't have to do anything to get it—but it also made his life very difficult.

Jack told his friend about the money. The friend advised Jack not to tell anyone at first. He told Jack to go to the bank and set up a retirement account. With a retirement account, Jack could set aside money for his old age. Unfortunately, Jack ignored his friend.

The first thing Jack did was tell his family, friends, and coworkers the good news. Then he claimed the money during a press conference. He told everyone he would donate most of the money to charity and help the poor. But he didn't do that.

Jack decided to accept the money in one single payment. Soon the money started pouring in . . . and so did the bills. He squandered (wasted) his money on vacations and nightclubbing. He threw his money around like it was nothing. He did buy a building that was worth a lot of money, but it burned down in a fire. It's hard to believe, but after a few years, Jack found himself owing money! He had spent everything.

Jack's story is not unique. Most lottery winners spend all of their earnings within five years.

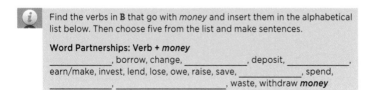

Find the verbs in **B** that go with *money* and insert them in the alphabetical list below. Then choose five from the list and make sentences.

Word Partnerships: Verb + *money*
_____, borrow, change, _____, deposit, _____, earn/make, invest, lend, lose, owe, raise, save, _____, spend, _____, _____, waste, withdraw *money*

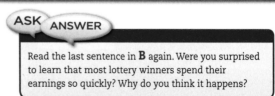

ASK ANSWER

Read the last sentence in **B** again. Were you surprised to learn that most lottery winners spend their earnings so quickly? Why do you think it happens?

2 Listening — Saving money, saving lives

CD 2
Track 23

A Read the question. Then listen to the news story and choose the best answer. Write down key words that helped you choose your answer.

What question is this introduction to the news story trying to answer?

a. Why are so many people going to the hospital?

b. Why do people in the hospital become ill?

c. Why are hospital stays so expensive?

key words: _____

CD 2
Track 24

B What is the problem? Listen to the rest of the story and fill in the missing words. Use no more than three words per blank.

The Problem

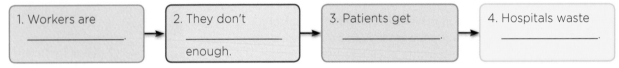

| 1. Workers are _____. | → | 2. They don't _____ enough. | → | 3. Patients get _____. | → | 4. Hospitals waste _____. |

CD 2
Track 24

C What is the solution to the problem? Listen again and fill in the missing words. Use no more than three words per blank.

The Solution

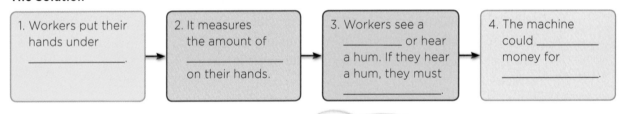

| 1. Workers put their hands under _____. | → | 2. It measures the amount of _____ on their hands. | → | 3. Workers see a _____ or hear a hum. If they hear a hum, they must _____. | → | 4. The machine could _____ money for _____. |

> **ASK** **ANSWER**
> What is the problem that many hospitals are facing? What is one possible solution? Use your answers in **B** and **C** to explain.

3 Reading — The San people and the monks

A What are some unusual ways that people have struck it rich?

B Look at the pictures and the title of the reading. How do you think these two groups have made money? Discuss your answers with a partner.

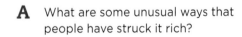
Southern Africa's San people

Greek monks

C Read the article. Circle *True* or *False*.

1. The San people won prize money.	True	False
2. The San know a lot about plants.	True	False
3. The new drug will make you hungry.	True	False
4. The monks play music in different styles.	True	False
5. The monks sing about world issues.	True	False
6. The monks squander their money.	True	False

Money from Unexpected Sources

The San people live in southern Africa. Scientists say that they may have been living there for as long as 40,000 years, hunting animals and gathering plants. Until recently, the once mighty San were broke and unemployed. They had lost their land and were no longer engaged in traditional activities, such as hunting. The few young San people with jobs were working as farm laborers. They were not learning about their ancient culture and language.

That may all change. The San have struck it rich. They recently signed an agreement with a large drug company. The San have traditional knowledge about plants that may be worth a lot of money. The drug company is especially interested in a particular cactus and how the San use it.

cactus

The San used to go on hunting trips. While away from home, they chewed on the cactus to decrease their appetite—they no longer felt hungry afterwards. Using the San's knowledge, the drug company plans to make a new drug from this plant. For people around the world who eat too much and have weight problems, this new drug could really help them by suppressing their appetites.

monastery

The San are being careful to use this "easy money" responsibly. Their first step will be to create jobs for their people. Their next priority will be education. Through education, they hope to save their culture and language for future generations.

When you think of a monk, you might think of a quiet man living in an isolated place. The "free monks" of Greece do live in a monastery, but they are anything but quiet. In fact, they sing. They have been recording their songs and selling many albums in Greece.

Young music listeners love to listen to the "free monks." Their songs are recorded in different styles (digital keyboard and rock, for example), and the themes are not only religious. The brothers also sing about problems like drugs and globalization.

The money from music sales hasn't exactly come pouring in, but the monks have made a profit. Some people are critical of this, but the monks are happy to accept the money. They set it aside for summer camps for teenagers. At the camps, the teens can play soccer and go horseback riding. The monks also donate money to other social programs that help many people.

D Complete the chart.

	the San	the monks
how they made money		
how they (will) spend it		

4 Language Link   Negative modals

A   Study the chart. Then match each negative modal
with its meaning below.

Negative modals
1. You **couldn't** have the winning ticket. I have it right here.
2. You **don't have to** make a lot of money to be happy.
3. You **may not** open a savings account with less than $100.
4. You **shouldn't** overuse your credit cards.
5. You**'d better not** spend any more money or you're going to be broke.
6. I **can't** balance a budget. I don't know how to do it.

a. It's not necessary.   d. It's not allowed.

b. I don't have the ability.   e. It's impossible.

c. It's not a good idea.   f. This is a warning.

B   Choose the best modal for each sentence.

1. A: Is that John over there?

   B: It may not / couldn't be. He's away in Paris this week.

2. You'd better not / don't have to be late because the bus leaves at exactly 2:00.

3. You have to / don't have to study for the test because it's been canceled.

4. You shouldn't / can't play the lottery. It's a waste of money.

5. You may / may not open a savings account if you want to.

6. You should / shouldn't open an account right now. Wait until next month.

7. Students couldn't / may not come to school without their uniforms. It's a rule.

8. You'd better not / can't drive without a driver's license. It's against the law.

9. If you've finished your exam, you'd better not / don't have to stay. It's OK to leave the room.

C   Choose one sentence in each pair that you agree with and share your ideas with a partner.

1. a. Everyone has to get married someday.

   b. You don't have to ever get married if you don't want to.

2. a. You should take a lot of risks in life, especially when you're young.

   b. You shouldn't take a lot of risks in life, even when you're young.

3. a. You'd better start saving money now or you won't have anything when you're older.

   b. You'd better not worry about money now or you'll get stressed.

5 Writing   **An experience with money**

A   Complete the title below with one of the verbs in the box. Then write about the experience.

> BORROWED   SAVED   MADE
> LOST   SPENT   WASTED

HOW I _____ A LOT OF MONEY

B   Exchange papers. What is the most interesting thing about your partner's experience?

HOW I LOST A LOT OF MONEY

One time, I lost a lot of money. I was only nine years old. My mother sent me to the corner store to buy something. She gave me a twenty-dollar bill and said, "I don't have anything smaller. Be careful with this and bring back all the change."

When I got to the store, I reached into my pocket. I couldn't find the money . . .

6 Communication   **A potential millionaire**

A   Use this survey form to interview your partner.

1. Do you usually finish something once you get started?	❑ yes	❑ no	
2. Do you know exactly how much you spend on food and clothes?	❑ yes	❑ no	
3. Are you single or married?	❑ single	❑ married	
4. How much of your salary do you save?	❑ none	❑ some	❑ a lot
5. Will you inherit a lot of money someday?	❑ yes	❑ no	
6. Do you usually shop at designer boutiques or discount stores?	❑ boutiques	❑ discount stores	
7. Do you like to negotiate prices?	❑ yes	❑ not really	
8. If you got lucky and won a lot of money in the lottery, what would you do with it?	❑ take a trip	❑ have a party	❑ invest it
9. How much sleep do you get each night?	❑ 5-6 hours	❑ 7-8 hours	❑ 8+ hours
10. When playing a game, do you get competitive and try to win?	❑ yes, always	❑ sometimes	❑ never

B   Compare your partner's answers with the actual millionaires' answers on page 154. How does your partner have similar habits to the millionaires? different habits? Is your partner a potential millionaire?

 Check out the World Link video.   Practice your English online at http://elt.heinle.com/worldlink

11 Honestly Speaking
Lesson A To tell the truth

1 Vocabulary Link   Tell me the truth.

A Look at the picture. Who are the people and what's happening? Read the
statements below the picture. Do you agree with them? Why or why not?

You shouldn't punish small children too severely if they tell a lie.
Learning to tell the truth is an important part of growing up.

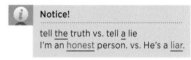

> **Notice!**
>
> tell the truth vs. tell a lie
> I'm an honest person. vs. He's a liar.

B Read the statements below. Notice the words in blue. Look up any expressions you don't know.
Then check the boxes that are true for you.

	Strongly agree	Agree	Disagree	Strongly disagree
1. Honesty is always best. There are no exceptions to this rule—I think it should always be followed.				
2. You should never lie if it's against the law. You could get arrested!				
3. You shouldn't tell the truth if it hurts someone's feelings. Do you want to make someone feel bad?				
4. The truth isn't always so clear—it's not really obvious.				
5. Sometimes I tell the truth and sometimes I don't. It depends on the circumstances. Each situation is different.				
6. Even telling a half truth is risky. It's just not worth doing.				

C Discuss your answers
with a partner.

> I strongly agree that honesty is
> always best. If you always tell the
> truth, you won't have any troubles.

> I don't know. Don't you think
> telling the truth depends on
> the circumstances? I mean, …

2 Listening An empty desk

A You are going to hear a conversation about a job résumé. When you prepare a résumé, what kind of information should be included? Make a list with a partner.

_____

_____

_____

CD 2
Track 25

B Listen. Check *True* or *False*. Correct the false sentences to make them true.

	True	False
1. Roger was fired.	☐	☐
2. Denise was sick last week.	☐	☐
3. There was a problem with Cindy's résumé.	☐	☐
4. Denise would never tell a half truth.	☐	☐
5. Denise is worried about the amount of work.	☐	☐
6. Interviewing is happening today.	☐	☐

CD 2
Track 26

C Listen. Complete the expressions with the missing words.

1. Well, _____, I don't know the details.

2. Uh-huh. She _____ her experience.

3. I agree. I don't think her boss was very happy that she had _____ him.

4. It's too bad, . . . but _____, I'm worried.

> **ASK ANSWER**
>
> What do you think of Cindy's punishment? Should she have been fired? Why or why not?

3 Pronunciation Repeating with rising intonation to show surprise

CD 2
Track 27

A Listen. Speaker B shows surprise by repeating a word that Speaker A says. Notice the rising intonation and stress. Then practice the conversations with a partner.

> **Conversation 1**
> A: Cindy was fired.
> B: She was fired? Why?
> A: Because she lied on her résumé.
> B: I can't believe it!

> **Conversation 2**
> A: Cindy got into trouble.
> B: She got into trouble? How?
> A: She dented her parents' car.
> B: You're kidding!

B Use these situations to make short conversations with a partner about Cindy like the ones in **A**. Remember to repeat with rising intonation to show surprise.

1. fail her exam / cheat on it

2. get a ticket / be caught speeding

3. move out / have an argument with her roommate

4 Speaking   **It's not cooked right.**

A Listen to the conversation. Where are Mr. and Mrs. Ward? What are they celebrating? What's the problem?

CD 2
Track 28

	Cooking meat:
i	rare
	medium rare
	medium
	well done

Mr. Ward: Happy Anniversary, honey.

Mrs. Ward: Same to you.

Mr. Ward: So, how's the chicken?

Mrs. Ward: Delicious. How about your steak?

Mr. Ward: It's all right . . .

Mrs. Ward: You don't sound very happy with it.

Mr. Ward: Well, it's not cooked right. I asked for medium rare. This is well done.

Mrs. Ward: Why don't you send it back?

Mr. Ward: Oh, I don't want to bother anyone. I can eat it, I guess.

Mrs. Ward: But it's expensive. I don't think you should eat it. Let's call the waiter.

B What would you say to the waiter? How would you complain? Write an ending to the conversation and practice it with a partner.

5 Speaking Strategy

A Read about each situation. Choose one to role play with a partner.

Student A: Assume the role of one of the friends or coworkers below.

Student B: Warn Student A about his or her actions. Use the Useful Expressions in the box to give strong opinions.

Your friend, who is a student in the U.S., often doesn't leave a big enough tip in restaurants.

Your coworker wastes a lot of time playing games on her computer.

Your friend, who doesn't like to study, often copies another friend's homework.

B Perform your dialog for the class.

> **Useful Expressions: Insisting**
>
> **If you don't** leave a bigger tip, the waiter **is going to** be upset.
>
> **I don't think you should** spend so much time playing games on your computer.
>
> **You have to** do your homework by yourself.

6 Language Link   Present unreal conditionals

A   Look at the photo and study what Hans said (the sentences in the chart).
Circle the correct answer to complete each sentence below.

My name is Hans. I live
in Austria. I'm a high
school student.

Present Unreal Conditionals	
If clause	**Result clause**
If I lived in Hawaii,	I would go to the beach every day.
If I were* a doctor,	I'd discover a cure for cancer.

* In conditional sentences, we use *were* for all subjects.

> *i*   You can also put the result
> clause first with no change
> in meaning:
>
> *I would go to the beach
> every day if I lived in Hawaii.*

1. Present unreal conditionals describe a situation that is
   true / not true right now.

2. The verb in the *if* clause is in the simple present / simple past.

3. *Would / Be* + base form is used in the result clause.

B   Read the sentences. Circle the answers that are true for you.

1. I'm / I'm not rich.

2. I'm / I'm not famous.

3. I have / don't have to study English.

4. I speak / don't speak English fluently.

5. I live / don't live with my parents.

6. I take / don't take a bus to school.

7. I have / don't have a lot of free time.

C   Now rewrite the sentences in **B** as present unreal conditionals.

1. _____

2. _____

3. _____

4. _____

5. _____

6. _____

7. _____

D   Share your answers with a partner. How are your answers different?

> If I were rich, I'd buy a big
> house in the suburbs.

> Really? I think if I were rich, I'd
> keep all my money safe in the bank.

7 Communication **Would you ever do this?**

A Look at these situations. Would you ever do any of these things?
Write *Y* for yes, *N* for no, or *M* for maybe.

Would you ever . . .

1. ____ eat a whole plate of food at a party?

2. ____ make free phone calls using a telephone card that you found?

3. ____ use the restroom in a cafe without actually buying anything there?

4. ____ stand and read an entire magazine in a store without buying it?

5. ____ download music, TV shows, or movies from the Internet without paying?

6. ____ take extra supplies from your office to use at home?

 B Discuss your answers in **A** with a partner.

I'd probably read an entire magazine without buying it. I guess it depends on the circumstances.

I'd definitely do it. Most magazines are too expensive!

 If you answered "yes," you can use *definitely* in your answer. If you answered "maybe," you might want to use *probably* in your answer.

Honestly Speaking

Lesson B   Who do you trust?

1   Vocabulary Link   I have confidence in . . .

A   Match items 1–6 with their definitions below. Two items have the same answer.

1. _____ I can't do it myself. I'm counting on you to help.

2. _____ He's a trustworthy employee. In two years, he's never been late to work.

3. _____ A truthful person doesn't lie on a résumé.

4. _____ I made a promise to you and I'm going to keep my word.

5. _____ I'm sure she'll get the job. I have confidence in her.

6. _____ I trust you. I know that you are telling the truth.

> Which combination with *trust* is incorrect? Cross it out.
>
> build trust
> earn trust
> learn to trust
> make trust

> a. dependable   c. relying on   e. do what you say you will do
> b. honest   d. believe in

B   Take this quiz.

1. Do you have to be truthful to succeed in life?

☐ yes   ☐ no

2. Do you typically trust strangers?

☐ yes   ☐ no

3. Do you have confidence in yourself and your abilities?

☐ yes   ☐ no

4. Do you always keep your word?

☐ yes   ☐ no

5. Who do you usually count on to give good personal advice?

_____

6. Who would you trust with a secret?

_____

C   Interview a partner using the questions in **B**. Ask and answer follow-up questions.

> Basically, I think you have to be truthful to be successful.

> I agree. You can lie sometimes, but sooner or later you're going to get caught.

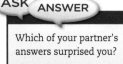

> **ASK   ANSWER**
>
> Which of your partner's answers surprised you?
>
> Which questions did you agree on?

2 Listening   I completely agree.

A You have 45 seconds. Read through the sentences below.

1. a. I agree. I trust her completely.

   b. I agree. Let's find someone else to do it.

2. a. You have to be patient. It takes time to earn someone's trust.

   b. You have to be patient. You can't learn to trust everyone.

3. a. I know. He really kept his word.

   b. I know. He didn't keep his word.

4. a. You can always count on her.

   b. Maybe you can count on her.

5. a. You're right. He's not so dependable.

   b. You're right. He's completely trustworthy.

CD 2
Track 29

B Listen and choose the best response from **A** to each sentence.

3 Reading   The kindness of strangers

A Have you ever been lost or stranded somewhere? What happened?

B Read the story on page 121 through line 18. What do you think will happen? Discuss your ideas with a partner.

C Read the entire story. Put the events in the order that they happened.

_____ A note was placed on the car.

_____ The car broke down.

_____ Philippe and Sophie had tea and local food.

_____ Philippe and Sophie went for a drive.

_____ A strange man showed up.

_____ The hired driver fixed the car.

_____ The hired driver left.

D Find these words in the reading.

1. Find a word in line 9 that means *sleep lightly*: _____

2. Find a word in line 9 that means *strange*: _____

3. Find a word in line 13 that means *showed with gestures*: _____

4. Find a word in line 15 that means *far away*: _____

5. Find a word in line 21 that means *smile*: _____

6. Find a word in line 26 that means *excited; very pleased*: _____

7. Find a word in line 30 that means *friendliness to guests*: _____

The Kindness of Strangers

You're cold and alone. You're afraid. You've lost your way. You can't speak the local language. You've lost your money and passport. You could experience any of these situations in another country. Who would you turn to for help?

5 My name is Philippe and my wife's name is Sophie. We're from France. Recently we were faced with a difficult situation while traveling by car in the mountains with our hired driver. It was going to be a long ride and we were tired. Just as we began to doze, the engine made an odd,
10 loud noise and then stopped working.

The sun was just setting and the air was getting cooler. We tried communicating with the driver but with little success. He pantomimed the act of going to get help and then he left.

15 We were in a remote location, with no houses in sight. We started to hear the cries of wild animals. Sophie was scared. We didn't have much food and it was getting colder, and darker. I began to lose confidence. Should we leave the car and seek shelter? Would our driver ever return? Was he a trustworthy man? We were very worried.

A couple of hours passed. Suddenly, the headlights from another car appeared in the dark. An
20 unfamiliar man got out of the car. He looked unfriendly at first, until his mouth opened with a big, friendly grin. He asked us to get into the car with him. He had such a kind face, and we knew we could count on him. We climbed into the car.

Before we left, he put a note on the windshield of the car with his phone number on it. Then he drove us to a nearby village, and we met his family. His cousin spoke basic French and
25 offered us tea and local foods. Everything was delicious. Everyone asked us questions and were thrilled to have unexpected guests.

Later that evening, the phone rang. It was our driver. He had kept his word and fixed the car. We prepared to leave and thanked our new friends. I couldn't believe the response from the cousin: "No, we thank *you* for coming into our home."

30 I will never forget the warmth and hospitality we received on that day because we relied on a complete stranger for help.

ASK ANSWER

Philippe and Sophie trusted a stranger. Would you have done the same thing? Have you ever helped a stranger? If so, what happened? If not, why not?

4 Language Link Reported statements

A Study the chart about reported statements. Notice how the verbs shift from the present to the past tense.

Reported statements	
You can use reported statements to report one person's statement to another. The use of *that* in the reported statement is optional.	
In the hospital, a patient talked to a nurse. Later, the nurse told the doctor what the patient said.	
Original statement	Reported statement
Patient to Nurse: I'm hungry.	Nurse to Doctor: Mr. Brown said (that) he was hungry.
P to N: I can't move my toes.	N to D: Mr. Brown said (that) he couldn't move his toes.
P to N: I will leave tomorrow.	N to D: He said (that) he would leave tomorrow.
P to N: My wife is coming today.	N to D: He said (that) his wife was coming today.

B Read Harold's online profile. What do you think of him? Tell a partner.

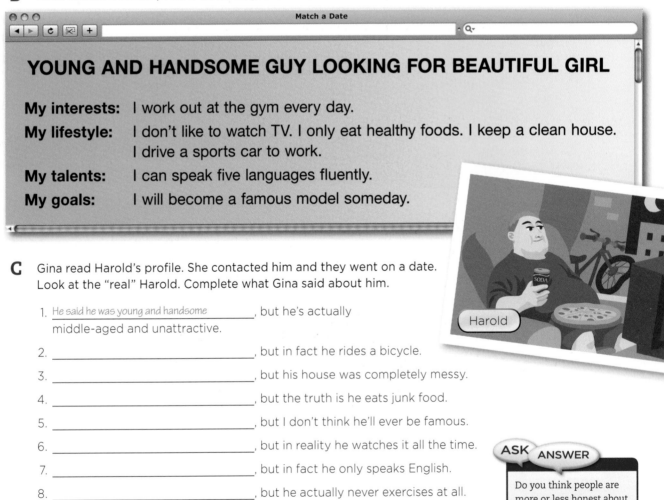

Match a Date

YOUNG AND HANDSOME GUY LOOKING FOR BEAUTIFUL GIRL

My interests: I work out at the gym every day.

My lifestyle: I don't like to watch TV. I only eat healthy foods. I keep a clean house. I drive a sports car to work.

My talents: I can speak five languages fluently.

My goals: I will become a famous model someday.

Harold

C Gina read Harold's profile. She contacted him and they went on a date. Look at the "real" Harold. Complete what Gina said about him.

1. *He said he was young and handsome*, but he's actually middle-aged and unattractive.
2. _____, but in fact he rides a bicycle.
3. _____, but his house was completely messy.
4. _____, but the truth is he eats junk food.
5. _____, but I don't think he'll ever be famous.
6. _____, but in reality he watches it all the time.
7. _____, but in fact he only speaks English.
8. _____, but he actually never exercises at all.

> **ASK ANSWER**
> Do you think people are more or less honest about themselves online? Why?

5 Writing I said that I was sick.

A Read "Caught in a Lie." What do you think happened? Finish the story with a partner.

B Write about a time you lied to make an excuse or to avoid hurting someone's feelings.

C Exchange papers with a partner. Read what happened. Was your partner caught in a lie?

> *CAUGHT IN A LIE*
>
> *A classmate invited me to go to the movies. I didn't want to go. I also didn't want to hurt his feelings. I said that I couldn't go to the movies. Even though I was fine, I said that I was sick.*
>
> *Later that same day, I went shopping with a friend. While we were shopping I unexpectedly . . .*

6 Communication My little white lie

A Look at these pictures. In each case, the person is telling "a white lie." What do you think a white lie is? Make a definition.

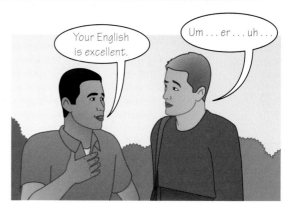

B With a partner, role play one of the situations in **A**. Be sure not to hurt the other person's feelings.

A: Your hair looks great!

B: Thanks. I like it, too.

A: Where did you get it done?

B: I did it myself.

A: Really? It looks like you went to an expensive salon.

 Check out the World Link video.

 Practice your English online at http://elt.heinle.com/worldlink

12 Our Earth

Lesson A   The natural world

1   Vocabulary Link   **Endangered animals**

A   Read about the koala. What is your school's mascot? Does your city or country have one? What other famous mascots do you know? Tell a partner.

> The koala is a national mascot of Australia. It lives in forested areas.
>
> It is endangered and could become extinct in 30 years. (The number of koalas has dropped from 100,000 in 2003 to probably less than 50,000 today.)
>
> As human beings move into forests, the koalas are suffering. They are forced to compete for food and this causes stress for them.

B   Read about Kiiza. Then complete the definitions below with the words in blue.

I have a new friend on Facebook. He lives in Uganda, Africa, with 15 family members. He loves to eat celery and bamboo. His home is a cloudy, misty, and cold forest with dense plant life. He's a baby now, but when he grows up he'll weigh 400 pounds. His name is Kiiza and he's a mountain gorilla.

In order to raise awareness that mountain gorillas are endangered, the Ugandan Wildlife Authority (UWA) has set up a Facebook account for the gorillas. When you befriend a gorilla online, you start receiving news about the gorillas. You can also donate money to protect them. There are only about 740 mountain gorillas remaining in the world, so it is crucial that we save them now.

With the money they raise, the UWA plans to install cameras in the forest so that people around the world can watch the gorillas and learn about them. The cameras will also discourage illegal hunting, which is the main reason the gorillas are decreasing in number.

C   Can you find a word or phrase in blue above that begins with . . .

1. "d" that means "thick?"
2. "e" that means "at risk?"
3. "e" that means "no longer living?"
4. "i" that means "against the law?"
5. "i" that means "put into position?"
6. "m" that means "a person / animal that represents a group of people?"

7. "m" that means "thin fog in the air?"
8. "r" that means "increase understanding?"
9. "r" that means "still existing?"
10. "s" that means "establish or create?"
11. "s" that means "feeling pain?"

D   Complete the chart with information about koalas and mountain gorillas. Write "NM" if the information isn't mentioned. Share your answers with a partner.

	Koalas	Mountain gorillas
How many there are		
Where they live		
What the problems are		
How they are being helped		

2 Listening — Rainforest animals

CD 2 Track 30

A Listen to four descriptions of rainforest animals. Circle the correct words to complete the definitions.

Listening 1   *Rodent* means dog / rat.
                 To exceed means to be greater / lesser than (an amount).

Listening 2   *Snout* means nose / legs.
                 Nocturnal means active / inactive at night.

Listening 3   *To camouflage* means to escape / to hide.
                 To inhabit means to eat / to live.

Listening 4   *An acrobat* does tricks on the ground / in the air.
                 To leap means to jump / to fall.

CD 2 Track 30

B Listen again. Number each photo. Can you match each description to the correct animal?

3 Pronunciation — Practice with pauses

A Read the information in the box. Then use slashes to indicate pauses in the sentences below.

> We organize our thoughts into groups of words. We mark these thought groups by pausing when we speak. You can insert a brief pause and a slight drop in intonation after:
>
> - prepositional, noun, and verb phrases
> - clauses
> - transitional phrases (e.g., *of course, finally*)
>
> *In the rain forest / you can see all kinds of animals / such as monkeys, / gorillas, / and jaguars.*

1. His home is a cloudy, misty, and cold forest with dense plant life.

2. He's a baby now, but when he grows up he'll weigh 400 pounds.

3. His name is Kiiza and he's a mountain gorilla.

4. With the money they raise, the UWA plans to install cameras in the forest so that people around the world can watch the gorillas and learn about them.

5. The gorillas, as you are aware, are endangered.

CD 2 Track 31

B Listen to the sentences in **A**.
Then practice saying the sentences with a partner.

4 Speaking   A summer job overseas

CD 2
Track 32

A Gustav and Carolina are international students. They're telling Bart about their summer work experience in the United States. Did they enjoy themselves?

Bart: So what exactly did you do over the summer?

Gustav: We worked as volunteers at Glacier National Park.

Bart: I've never been there. What's it like?

Carolina: It's beautiful. There are mountains and lakes . . . and, of course, glaciers!

Bart: How was the job?

Gustav: We had to do a lot of physical work. It was kind of hard.

Carolina: That's true, but it was exciting, too! We actually saw bears!

Bart: Wow! That *does* sound exciting. Maybe I should apply. I'll need a job next summer.

Carolina: Sorry, Bart, but you can't apply to that program. It's a special program for international students.

B Practice the conversation in groups of three.

5 Speaking Strategy

A Imagine that you and your partner are looking for a place to live together as roommates. Write down some of the important things to consider.

_____ *cost* _____

_____

_____

_____

> **ASK** **ANSWER**
>
> If you could work overseas for the summer, where would you go? What would you do?

Useful Expressions
Offering another opinion
That's true, but . . .
Yes, but on the other hand . . .
Even so . . .
But then again . . .

B Read about these two possible places to live. Add 2-4 more ideas to the lists. With a partner, discuss their positive and negative aspects. Use the Useful Expressions to help you.

City apartment	Suburban home
expensive	big backyard
near public transportation	need a car
small bedrooms	quiet neighborhood
big balcony with a great view	nothing to do on weekends

> The apartment in the city is expensive.

C With your partner, choose one of the locations in **B**. Tell the class which location you chose and why.

> That's true, but living in the city is exciting. There's so much to do!

6 Language Link   *Like* as a preposition and verb

A   Study the chart. Notice the different uses of the word *like*. Which ones are you familiar with? Which sentences have the same or similar meanings?

Like as a preposition or conjunction	*Like* as a verb (phrase)
It's <u>just</u> like my jacket.	I like to sing karaoke with my friends.
It <u>looks</u> like my jacket.	I like singing karaoke with my friends.
I prefer fresh fruits like apples and oranges.	I feel like seeing a movie.
There's <u>nothing</u> like a bowl of fresh fruit.	I'd like to see a movie.

B   Match each question with an appropriate response.

> **Remember!**
> What's she like? She's a little shy.

1. Did you feel like walking the dog?
2. Do you like to walk your dog?
3. What does your dog look like?
4. Would you like to walk the dog?
5. What's your dog like?

a. He's white with black spots.
b. He's really friendly.
c. No, I didn't but I did it anyway.
d. Sure. I can do it.
e. No, I don't. It's a pain.

C   Read about a country. Then, with a partner, ask and answer the questions.

1. What language do they speak there?
2. What do tourists say about the environment?
3. What's the weather like?
4. Who are the Maori people?
5. What fruits do they grow?
6. What does their money look like?
7. What sport do the people like to watch and play?

English is the official language. There is a lot of nature here: it has mountains, beaches, lakes, and unique wildlife. Travelers say it is safe and beautiful. The original inhabitants, the Maori people, are from Polynesia. The country has lots of sunshine and rain. They grow many fruits here, such as mandarin oranges and kiwi fruit. Many of the four million residents enjoy watching and playing rugby. Their fifty-cent coin has a picture of Queen Elizabeth II on it. For a great vacation destination, there's nothing like it!

D   Guess the name of the country. Would you like to visit there? Why or why not? Check your answer on page 154.

7 Communication   What in the world?

A   Work alone. Take this quiz.

harbor

volcano

cave

coastline

What / Where is the world's . . .

1. **busiest harbor?**
   a. Singapore
   b. Pusan (South Korea)
   c. Hong Kong (China)

2. **largest island?**
   a. Great Britain
   b. Greenland (Denmark)
   c. Honshu (Japan)

3. **highest waterfall?**
   a. Tugela Falls (South Africa)
   b. Angel Falls (Venezuela)
   c. Sutherland Falls
      (New Zealand)

4. **oldest active volcano?**
   a. Kilauea (USA)
   b. Yasur (Vanuatu)
   c. Etna (Italy)

5. **longest mountain range?**
   a. the Austrian Alps (Europe)
   b. the Andes (South America)
   c. the Urals (Europe)

6. **longest cave?**
   a. Mammoth Cave (USA)
   b. Hollach Cave (Switzerland)
   c. Sistema Ox Bel Ha (Mexico)

7. **deepest lake?**
   a. Lake Superior (USA / Canada)
   b. Lake Nyasa (Africa)
   c. Lake Baikal (Russia)

8. **largest desert?**
   a. the Sahara (North Africa)
   b. the Australian (Australia)
   c. the North American
      (Mexico / USA)

9. **longest coastline?**
   a. Australia
   b. Canada
   c. Chile

B   Work in groups of four. Imagine that you are on a quiz show.

Student A: quiz show announcer

Student B–D: quiz show contestants

1. Announcer: Read a question from the quiz in **A**.

2. Contestants: Write down your answer on a piece of paper. Then hold your paper up and show the group.

3. Announcer: Check the answer on page 154. Give each contestant 1 point for a correct answer. Continue asking questions.

4. Contestants: The person with the most points at the end of the game wins.

ASK ANSWER

Which of the places in **A** would you most like to visit? least like to visit? Why? What do you think the place is like?

Our Earth

Lesson B   The man-made world

1   Vocabulary Link   Great structures

 A   First look at the pictures of these great structures. What do you know about them? Read about them and then answer the questions with a partner.

1. Where do you think these structures are located?

2. What do they connect?

3. What were some of the challenges faced in building them?

Akashi Kaikyo Bridge

Channel Tunnel

Before it was built, people traveled between Honshu and Awaji Island by ferry. Now this bridge links the two islands. There were several obstacles to building the bridge. For example, the builders had to consider the weather (high winds and heavy rain). To get around these problems, engineers made a strong bridge that allows the wind to pass through it. The bridge can also withstand earthquakes.

In 1802, French engineer Albert Mathieu proposed building a tunnel across the English channel. It wasn't until 1988, however, that construction on the "Chunnel" began. Tunneling underwater was a major engineering challenge. There are actually three tubes in the Chunnel. Two tubes accommodate trains while a third is an escape route. Trains transport both goods and people through the tunnel.

Complete the chart below	
accommodate	
	consideration
construct	
	proposition
	transportation

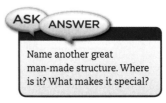

ASK ANSWER

Name another great man-made structure. Where is it? What makes it special?

B   Write each blue word in **A** next to its definition below.

1. think about; study _____*consider*_____

2. to carry from place to place _____

3. suggested _____

4. to resist _____

5. things that prevent success _____

6. the act of making something _____

7. to make space for _____

8. connects _____

9. the road or path you use to get to a place _____

10. things that are sold to consumers _____

11. pipes _____

12. to solve (a problem) _____

2 Listening An engineer's job

A Look at this list of words. Which ones do you know? With a partner, look up any unfamiliar words in your dictionary.

> access   architect   blueprint   edge   investigate   leaky

CD 2
Track 33

B Listen to this interview with Jamie Marsh. Which picture shows what she does in her job? Listen and circle the correct one.

CD 2
Track 33

C Listen. Complete these sentences about Jamie's job. Discuss with a partner.

1. Jamie works with _____ buildings.
2. She checks problems so that they don't _____ mistakes.
3. Rapelling is a way to get access to _____ places.
4. After you hook up to the top of the building, you _____ over the edge.
5. Rapelling is scary, but you can get _____.

3 Reading Building down

A What should be done about overcrowding in cities? Discuss with a partner.

B Read the interview with Erika Van Beek, an engineer, on page 131.
Then write the questions below in the correct spaces.

> a. ~~Well, in some places there simply isn't any land left for building, right?~~
>
> b. Isn't "building down" more dangerous than other kinds of construction?
>
> c. Isn't it expensive?
>
> d. What do you think is the biggest problem facing our cities?
>
> e. What would you say to people who doubt your idea?
>
> f. Think creatively? What do you suggest?

What country is building a series of islands to look like a map of the world?
a. China
b. the United Arab Emirates
c. the United States

THE FUTURE BUILDING BOOM?

1 _____

I think it's overcrowding. Talk to anyone living in a major metropolitan area and they will say the same thing: there's no space. Even the suburbs are getting crowded.

2 _Well, in some places there simply isn't any land left for building, right?_

Yes, that's true, but you have to think creatively. You can't give up so easily.

3 _____

What I'm saying is that we can build more structures underground. We can add parking lots, malls, hotels, and even apartment buildings. There's plenty of space.

4 _____

Yes, it can be. In the past, building underground has been very expensive. However, we have new technology that will bring the cost down. It involves using robots, which are great because you don't have to pay them a salary!

5 _____

Actually, I think it's safer than building skyscrapers, for example. Remember, we already do it. We have subways and underground shopping malls. I'm just suggesting we invest in a variety of bigger projects and that we dig deeper.

6 _____

I can understand their feelings. Whenever there's a new idea, it can cause controversy. But "building down" is not some kind of impractical idea. It makes sense. There is so much space underground that can accommodate a lot of traffic, storage, and people. With the new technology we have, we'd be crazy not to consider the idea—it's the wave of the future!

C Check (✔) the statements you think Erika would agree with.

1. ☐ We should focus on building more skyscrapers.

2. ☐ Building underground is a practical solution to overcrowding.

3. ☐ New technology can make building underground more affordable.

4. ☐ Robots are a cheap and safe alternative to using people.

5. ☐ We should limit underground projects to subways and shopping malls.

D Look at the pronouns in red above. What do they refer to?
Write your answers.

1. Yes, it can be. _____

2. It involves using robots . . . _____

3. . . . you don't have to pay them a salary. _____

4. Remember, we already do it. _____

5. . . . it can cause controversy. _____

6. It makes sense. _____

ASK ANSWER

What do you think of the idea of "building down"? Do you like the idea of working, shopping, or living underground? Why or why not?

4 Language Link   The passive with various tenses

A Read this information about skyscrapers. Study the verbs in the chart.

	Active	Passive
simple present	Engineers build skyscrapers with a steel frame.	Most skyscrapers are built with a steel frame.
simple past	The Woolworth Company built a skyscraper in 1913.	One of the first skyscrapers was built in 1913.
present perfect	Engineers have built the world's tallest building in Dubai.	The world's tallest building has been built in Dubai.
future with *will*	Someday they will build a skyscraper without concrete.	Someday a skyscraper without concrete will be built.

B Here are some facts about three engineering feats. Complete the sentences with the verb in parentheses. Use the passive form that is indicated.

Itaipu Dam

simple past   1. The dam _____was completed_____ (complete) in 1991.

present perfect 2. It _____ (visit) by more than 9 million people.

Akashi Kaikyo Bridge

simple present 3. The record for the longest suspension bridge _____ (hold) by the Akashi Kaikyo Bridge.

simple past   4. The bridge _____ (design) to be 12,825 feet but it _____ (stretch) even longer after a big earthquake.

present perfect 5. The bridge _____ (finish) for many years.

Chunnel

simple past   6. The first passengers on a Chunnel train were surprised when they _____ (transport) to the other side in only 20 minutes.

future with *will* 7. In the future, experts predict that even more passengers _____ (carry) through the Chunnel.

5 Writing   A famous landmark

A What famous architectural landmarks do you know? Choose one and write about it.

B Exchange papers with a partner. Ask questions about your partner's landmark.

> ### THE HAGIA SOPHIA
> The Hagia Sophia is interesting because it tells a lot about my country's history. It was built in the year 360. It has been damaged by wars, earthquakes, and fires, but it has always been rebuilt.
> The building was originally a church. Then it was a mosque. Now it is a popular museum . . .

6 Communication — What is best for our city?

 A Look at the picture and read about the problems facing Diamond City. What projects have been proposed to solve problems? Use your own words to discuss each situation with a partner.

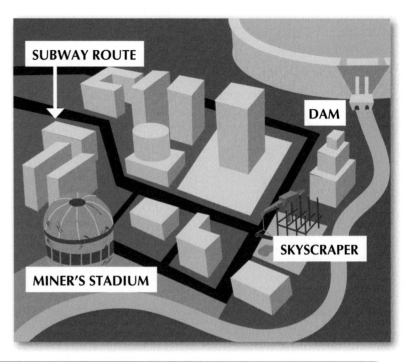

SUBWAY ROUTE

DAM

SKYSCRAPER

MINER'S STADIUM

Problem 1: The dam was built 30 years ago, but it is weak.

Project: Repair the dam. It will take at least five years to repair.

Notes: The city has been hit by a huge flood about every 100 years. The last flood was 80 years ago and the downtown area was destroyed.

Problem 2: The traffic is terrible in Diamond City. Businesses are leaving the city due to the traffic congestion.

Project: Build a new subway line to limit traffic congestion. It will take at least 10 years to finish.

Notes: Digging in the soft, sandy ground is difficult and expensive, but a new subway system is necessary for this pressing problem.

Problem 3: The baseball stadium has been used for 20 years.

Project: Repair the stadium. It will take at least five years to repair.

Notes: The Diamond City Miners baseball team is the city's biggest moneymaker. However, if the stadium isn't fixed in three years, the team may move to another city.

Problem 4: Diamond City's economy has not been performing well for the last 15 years.

Project: Build a new skyscraper to attract businesses to the city. It will take eight years to finish.

Notes: The skyscraper will be built on an abandoned lot. The construction will be dangerous and expensive.

 B Work in groups of 3 or 4 and rank the projects in the order you would do them. Follow these rules:

- A new project can be started only after the previous one has been finished.
- The group must agree on the order for doing the projects.

 Check out the World Link video.   Practice your English online at http://elt.heinle.com/worldlink

Review: Units 10-12

1 Storyboard

A Lisa is asking Sara about her recent vacation. Look at the pictures and complete the conversations. More than one answer may be possible for each blank.

B Practice the conversation with a partner. Then change roles and practice again.

C What do you think of Sara's idea? What would you do to raise awareness? Tell a partner.

2 See It and Say It

A Study the picture for ten seconds and then close your book.
With a partner, take turns describing the scene in as much detail as you can.

B Look at the picture again. Answer the questions with a partner.

1. Who are these people? Where are they?

2. Where are they going or what are they looking for? What time of day is it?

3. What do you think the leader is thinking?

C What would you do if you were the leader of the group?
Make suggestions and explain your answers.

> It's getting late. They should stop. If I were the leader, I'd suggest we sleep in the cave.

> That's one idea. But then again, I think the cave would be too cold. I'd suggest . . .

3 Polly and Patsy

A Read this story about Polly and Patsy. Fill in the missing words.

Polly and Patsy are sisters. They both _____ it rich by _____ the lottery.

Polly decided she could _____ by on very little money. She made a very tight budget for herself. She took 50% of the money and _____ it to charities. She also _____ aside the _____ amount in a retirement _____.

Patsy, on the other hand, did something different. She _____ her money on food, vacations, and presents for herself. She spent way _____ much money and didn't _____ anything. In one year she had _____ into debt and _____ afford to pay _____ all the money she had borrowed.

B With a partner, compare your answers in **A**.

C Imagine your friend has won the lottery. Give him or her some financial advice. Use the negative modals in the box.

> don't have to   had better not   shouldn't

> *Well, for one thing, you don't have to tell everyone right away.*

4 Listening

CD 2
Track 34

Listen to each response. Then choose the correct question for the response.

1. a. ☐ What does she look like?
   b. ☐ What's she like?

2. a. ☐ Why did you buy a new car?
   b. ☐ Why do you want a new car?

3. a. ☐ What would you do if you won the contest?
   b. ☐ What will you do when you win the contest?

4. a. ☐ Did you like the painting?
   b. ☐ How long did it take you to paint it?

5. a. ☐ When did they complete the bridge?
   b. ☐ When will they complete the bridge?

6. a. ☐ What do you usually do on Friday night?
   b. ☐ What do you want to do on Friday night?

5 While You Were Out

Imagine that, while your boss was out, you took several messages. Using reported speech, give the messages to your boss. Then switch roles.

Student A: Give these messages to your boss.

1. Mary: "The meeting is scheduled for 2:00."

2. Tom: "I won't be in the office next week. I'll be in Milan on business."

3. Copy company: "We're running behind schedule on your job."

Student B: Give these messages to your boss.

1. Celine: "I can't make the deadline."

2. Dry cleaners: "Your suits are ready."

3. Mario: "I don't understand your memo. I have questions about it."

> Were there any messages while I was out?

> Yes. There were three. Mary called. She said that...

6 Making Plans

A With a partner, choose a situation and create a conversation of eight to ten sentences.

Situation 1	Situation 2
Partner A: There's a Broadway show in town, and your partner wants to see it. You think the show is too expensive.	Partner A: There's a popular art exhibit at the museum. Your partner wants to see it. You think it will be very crowded and hard to see the paintings.
Partner B: There's a Broadway show in town and you really want to see it. Persuade your partner to go.	Partner B: There's an exhibition at the museum in town and you really want to see it. Persuade your partner to go.

B: I really want to see the Broadway show that's in town.

A: Yes, but it's too expensive.

B: That's true, but . . .

B Practice your conversation. Then perform it for another pair.

Language Summaries

Unit 1 Indoors and Outdoors

Lesson A

Vocabulary Link

combine
do repairs
home improvement
neutral
option
overwhelming
rearrange
work well (together)

Additional Vocabulary

reorganize

Speaking Strategy

Making Informal Suggestions

Why don't you fix it yourself?
Have you thought about fixing it
    yourself?
I know what you should do. Call
    my friend.
Try calling my friend.

**Responding to Informal
Suggestions**

Good idea!
That's a good idea.
Sounds good to me.
I guess it's worth a try.
Maybe I'll do that.
I don't think so.
No, I don't like that idea . . .

Lesson B

Vocabulary Link

public
the general public
open to the public

privacy
have (no) privacy

public / private
~ conversation, ~ figure, ~ life,
~ school, in ~

publicly / privately
~ owned business

disturb
none of your business
rights

Unit 2 Life's Changes

Lesson A

Vocabulary Link

kid
teen
(young) adult
grown-up
childhood
adolescence
adulthood
start a family

Additional Vocabulary

the elderly/the youth
the rich/the poor
the employed/
    the unemployed

Speaking Strategy

Talking about plans
I'm planning to rent a car.
I'm going to visit my cousins.
I'm thinking about taking a trip.

Talking about needs
I need (to get) a new driver's
    license.

Lesson B

Vocabulary Link

be born
buy a house
enroll (in college)
fall in love
get a job
get divorced
get married
get pregnant
go to school
have children
leave home
raise a family
retire

Unit 3 Getting Information

Lesson A

Vocabulary Link

argue/get into an argument
chat/have a (nice) chat
discuss/have a long
  discussion
gossip
share
strike up a conversation
carry on a conversation
talk/give a talk
send messages

Speaking Strategy

Interrupting someone politely

Introducing yourself
Excuse me. May I interrupt for
  a moment? My name is . . .
  and I wanted to say . . .

I'm sorry to interrupt. / I beg your
  pardon. I just wanted to
  introduce myself. My name
  is . . .

Interrupting someone you know
Excuse me. Sorry to bother you,
  (name), but I have a question.

Could I interrupt for a second?
  I just wanted to say . . .

Lesson B

Vocabulary Link

news
get (your) news
hear the news
tell someone the news
in the news
a (juicy) piece of news
news source
cable/(nightly) network news
local/national/international news
entertainment news
morning news program

media
in the media
new/traditional media

word of mouth

Additional Vocabulary

reliable/unreliable
accurate/inaccurate

Unit 4 Men and Women

Lesson A

Vocabulary Link

get a haircut/a manicure/
  a tattoo/your ears
  pierced
wear makeup/a skirt/bright
  colors
brush your hair/teeth
chip your nail/tooth
color your hair/nails
straighten your hair/teeth
wash your face/hair

Additional Vocabulary

dye your hair
have plastic surgery
shave your head

Speaking Strategy

Disagreeing politely
I agree up to a point.
Yes, but . . . / I know, but . . .
I'm not sure. / I don't know.
I'm not sure it's/that's (such) a
  good idea.
I see what you're saying, but . . .
But what about (the cost)?

Lesson B

Vocabulary Link

ask (someone) out
break up
cheat on
get along
get over
go out
grow up
run into
turn (someone) down
turn on (the TV)

Additional Vocabulary

pretend

Unit 5 Being Different

Lesson A

Vocabulary Link

good/bad behavior
appropriate/inappropriate
considerate/inconsiderate
honest/dishonest
kind/unkind
polite/impolite
pleasant/unpleasant
respectful/disrespectful
responsible/irresponsible

Speaking Strategy
Asking about customs

Is it OK to use my fingers?
    Please, go right ahead.
    Absolutely.

    Actually, it's probably better to
        use a fork.
    Normally, people use a fork.

Is it all right to wear shoes inside?
    Sure, no problem.
    Yeah, it's fine.

    Actually, you should take off
        your shoes.
    No, you really should take off
        your shoes.

Lesson B

Vocabulary Link

body language
eating habits
eye contact
facial expression
jet lag
language barrier
personal space
small talk

Unit 6 Big Business

Lesson A

Vocabulary Link

advertise/advertisement/
    advertiser
consume/consumption
    consumer
develop/development/
    developer
employ/employment/
    employer/employee
invest/investment/investor
manage/management/
    manager
produce/production/
    producer
promote/promotion/
    promoter
purchase
ship/shipment/shipper

Additional Vocabulary

find/see (natural wonders)
grow (fruits, vegetables)
import/export (food, gas,
    products)
make/produce (cars, electronics)
raise (animals, children)
speak (languages)

Speaking Strategy
Emphasizing important points

I'd like to emphasize that . . .
Never forget that . . .
This is a key point . . .
The bottom line is . . .

Lesson B

Vocabulary Link

a steady decline/decline steadily
a sharp fall/fall sharply
a slight rise/rise slightly
a dramatic increase/increase
    dramatically
(be) up/(be) down
get better/get worse
increase/decrease
recover
in a slump

Additional Vocabulary

typical/atypical
simple/complex
sincere/insincere
positive/negative
convincing/unconvincing

Unit 7 Health

Lesson A

Vocabulary Link

dizzy	chew
drowsy	cough
exhausted	shiver
weak/weakness	swallow
blink	make sense
breathe/breathing	

Additional Vocabulary

high/low blood pressure
nauseous
a rash
scratch
sneeze
symptom
mild/severe
common/rare

Speaking Strategy

Giving serious advice
In my opinion, you should . . .
I always advise people to . . .
I think the best idea (for you)
    is to . . .
If I were you, I'd . . .

Accepting advice
You're right. Thanks for the advice.
That makes (a lot of) sense. I'll give
    it a try.
I'll try it and get back to you.

Refusing advice
I'm not sure that would work for
    me.
That doesn't (really) make sense
    to me.
I could never do that.

Lesson B

Vocabulary Link

sick: make someone ~,
    call in ~, ~ day,
    ~ of (something/
    someone), worried ~
homesick, airsick, carsick,
lovesick, seasick

care: take ~ of, ~ about

well: do ~, ~ behaved, ~ paid,
might (may) as ~

boss around
cut class
ground (= punish) someone
treat (someone) like (a kid)

Additional Vocabulary

chaos	fatigue
gentle	straightforward
tidy	

Unit 8 Sports and Hobbies

Lesson A

Vocabulary Link

activity: be involved in/
participate in an ~,
spare time/leisure time ~
physical ~, outdoor ~

active: stay/remain ~,
~ member

action: where the ~ is,
take ~

athlete: serious ~,
professional ~

Additional Vocabulary

renew (=begin again OR
    =extend a time period)

Speaking Strategy

Talking about a game
It's played with . . .
You don't need any special
    equipment.
There are 11 players on each
    team. / You are competing
    against each other.
One team starts by . . . / The
    game begins when . . .
The team with the most points
    wins. / The object is to score
    the most runs.
It's played on a field. / It's
    played all over the world.

Lesson B

Vocabulary Link

verb + preposition

ask for	pay for
believe in	prepare for
deal with	run on
dream of	stay in
happen to	stay with
head out	wake up
know about	warn about

verb + object + preposition
ship (something) by
spend (something) on
thank (someone) for

Unit 9 Social Issues

Lesson A

Vocabulary Link

expand
launch (v)
make progress
raise taxes
reelect
tax (v)
vow (v)
candidate
citizen
corporation
term
as usual
clear (adj)
enthusiastically

vote
~ for, ~ against
voting age

up for reelection

Additional Vocabulary

campaign
never in my wildest dreams
running neck and neck
give it your best shot
a record turnout

Speaking Strategy

Language for presentations

Stating the purpose
Today, I'd like to talk to you
    about . . .
I'll begin by (talking about the
    issue). / I'll provide an
    overview of (the issue).
Then I'll list the (two/three/four) . . .

Stating important points
Let's talk first about . . .
One of the main causes (of rush
    hour traffic) is . . .
Another/A second cause of . . . is . . .
And finally . . .

Lesson B

Vocabulary Link

destroy/destruction
develop/development
encourage/encouragement
force/force
improve/improvement
protect/protection
provide
rely/reliance
support/support
waste/waste

spread
~ quickly, ~ a rumor, ~ the news,
~ jam (on toast)

Additional Vocabulary

suburban
urban
a change of scene
put down roots
wait and see

Unit 10 Having It All

Lesson A

Vocabulary Link

(can't) afford   go into debt
broke   owe
get by   pay back
short on money

insert
put away
select

next to nothing
way too much

Additional Vocabulary

rich in (full of)
rich (interesting and colorful)
poor (expressing sympathy)
poor (below average)

Speaking Strategy

Apologizing

Small accident or mistake
I'm sorry. It was an accident.
Sorry. My mistake.
I can't believe I did that.

Serious accident or mistake
I'm really sorry that I forgot to . . .
I'm so sorry about damaging . . .
I want to apologize for what
    happened.

Accepting an apology
Don't worry about it.
Oh, that's OK.
No problem. It happens.
Apology accepted.

Lesson B

Vocabulary Link

adjective + money
easy ~, prize ~, worth (a lot of) ~

verb + money
accept ~, claim ~, donate ~,
set aside ~, squander ~,
throw ~ around

money + verb
~ pours in

earnings
retirement account
strike it rich

Unit 11 Honestly Speaking

Lesson A

Vocabulary Link

an honest person/a liar
tell a lie/tell the truth
against the law
depends on the
    circumstances
exception
half truth
hurt someone's feelings
punish
obvious
(not) worth doing

Additional Vocabulary

to be honest
in all honesty
lie to (someone)
lie about (something)

Speaking Strategy

Insisting
If you don't leave a bigger tip, the
    waiter is going to be upset.
I don't think you should spend so
    much time playing games on
    your computer.
You have to do your homework
    by yourself.

Lesson B

Vocabulary Link

count on
have confidence in
keep your word
trustworthy
truthful

trust
build ~, earn ~, learn to ~

Additional Vocabulary

doze   (panto)mime
grin   remote
odd   thrilled

Unit 12 Our Earth

Lesson A

Vocabulary Link

dense
endangered
(become) extinct
illegal
install
mascot
misty
raise awareness
remaining
set up
suffer

Additional Vocabulary

cave
coastline
volcano
harbor

Speaking Strategy

Offering another opinion

That's very nice, but . . .
Yes, but on the other hand . . .
Even so . . .
But then again . . .

Lesson B

Vocabulary Link

accommodate/accommodation
consider/consideration
constuct/construction
propose/proposition
transport/transportation
get around
link (v)
withstand
goods
obstacle
route
tube

Additional Vocabulary

access
architect
blueprint
edge
investigate
leaky

Grammar Notes

Unit 1 Indoors and Outdoors

Lesson A **Language Link:** Participles used as adjectives

I can't get a copy of the report right now. The printer is **jammed**.	Past participles describe a state.
How do you clean a **flooded** <u>basement</u>? Call the plumber. The kitchen drain <u>is</u> **clogged**.	Past participles of verbs (-*ed* forms) can be used as adjectives. Most can come before the noun or after a linking verb (*be, seem*, etc.).
One pipe is **bent** and the other one is **broken**.	Many verbs have irregular simple past and past participle forms (not formed with -*ed* ending).

Past participles used as adjectives					
Present	Past	Past Participle	Present	Past	Past Participle
bend	bent	**bent**	crack	cracked	**cracked**
broke	broke	**broken**	flood	flooded	**flooded**
burn	burned	**burned**	freeze	froze	**frozen**
clog	clogged	**clogged**	jam	jammed	**jammed**

Lesson B **Language Link:** Expressing prohibition

You **can** park here for free. You**'re not allowed to** blog about your job online. Sharp objects **aren't permitted** in your carry-on bags.	Use *can, allowed to*, or *permitted* to give or deny permission.
You **must not** eat anything before your physical exam. Children **can't** ride the roller coaster by themselves.	Use *must (not)* for formal rules and warnings. It is more common to use *can't* (rather than *mustn't*) for prohibition in spoken English.
We**'re supposed to** hand in our assignments today. Shhh! You**'re not supposed to** talk in the library.	*Be supposed to* means "be expected to." Use *be supposed to* for a rule that you should follow.
No swimming or **diving** (allowed).	*No* + gerund (verb + -*ing*) is used on signs to say something is prohibited.

Unit 2 Life's Changes

Lesson A Language Link: Review of future forms

She**'ll** do well in her new job. I'm tired. I think I**'ll** go to bed.	*Will* is used for • general predictions • decisions made at the moment of speaking.
She**'s going to** do well in her new job. I**'m going to** fly to Costa Rica for the holidays. Look at all the traffic! We**'re going to** be late!	*Be going to* is used for • general predictions • future plans / intentions • situations when you can see / hear something is about to happen.
I**'m having** lunch with some clients at 1:00.	The present continuous is used for • future plans that have already been made.
The movie **starts** in ten minutes. Hurry up!	The simple present is used for • scheduled events in the near future.

Lesson B Language Link: Modals of future possibility

Class **may/might/could** end early tomorrow.	Use *may*, *might* or *could* to talk about future possibility.

Is he going to lose his job?
   He **may/might/could**. It depends.
Will you be home by 8:00 tonight?
   I **may/might (be)**. I'm not really sure.
	Also use *may*, *might*, or *could* to answer questions about the future.

Are you going to attend the party? I **may/might not**. I'm not feeling well.	To answer in the negative, use *may* or *might* (but not *could*).

Unit 3 Getting Information

Lesson A Language Link: Participial and prepositional phrases

I'm looking for Lee Moore. Is he the man **wearing the suit**? No, that's not him. Lee's the tall guy **with the mustache**.	You can identify people with participial and prepositional phrases.
My boss is the woman **chatting on the phone**. Can you see the person **standing first in line**?	A present participle is a verb + *-ing*. It follows the noun it's modifying.
John is the man **by the door**. She's the girl **in the glasses**.	A prepositional phrase starts with *in*, *on*, *by*, etc. It also follows the noun it's modifying.

Lesson B Language Link: Review of the present perfect

I'm a reporter at the Daily News. I**'ve worked** there for a long time.	Use the present perfect for actions that began in the past and continue in the present.
I**'ve known** her <u>for</u> 15 years. I**'ve known** her <u>since</u> 1996.	Use the present perfect with *for* (for a period of time) and *since* (for a point in time).
I**'ve known** her <u>since</u> I was a child.	You can also use *since* before a time clause.
<u>How long</u> **have** you **lived** here? All my life.	Use *how long* to ask about a period of time.
Have you **heard** the big news? I**'ve met** you once before.	Use the present perfect for past actions when the time they happened isn't important.

Unit 4 Men and Women

Lesson A Language Link: The present perfect with *already*, *just*, *never*, *still* and *yet*

I **haven't started** my homework <u>yet</u>, but Mark **has done** his <u>already</u>.	The present perfect is used for past events that are connected to the present. Adverbs emphasize the meaning of the sentence.
I**'ve** <u>already</u> **bought** some clothes for my trip.	Use *already* in affirmative sentences to say you've completed something. Questions with *already* can indicate surprise that an action has been completed.
Have you <u>already</u> **finished** your homework?	
Have you **made** your vacation plans <u>yet</u>? My boss **hasn't approved** my time off <u>yet</u>.	Use *yet* in questions and negative sentences for expected actions that have not been finished.
They <u>still</u> **haven't** called. (= They haven't called yet.)	Use *still* in negative sentences to indicate something hasn't happened yet.
I don't know him well. Actually, we**'ve** <u>just</u> **met**.	Use *just* for an action that happened recently in the past.
I**'ve** <u>never</u> **traveled** abroad. **Have** you <u>ever</u> **been** on TV?	*Never* = at no time in the past (with affirmative statements) *Ever* = at any time in the past up to now (with questions and negative statements)

Lesson B Language Link: Phrasal verbs

I **work out** every morning.	Phrasal verbs (verb + particle) have two or three words.
Do you want to **watch** (= look at) TV? **Watch out** (= be careful)! There's a car coming!	When the verb is followed by a particle (a preposition or adverb), the meaning often changes.
I can't **figure** this problem **out**. I can't **figure out** this problem.	Some phrasal verbs can be "separated" by a noun object. The noun can also follow the phrasal verb.
I can't **figure** it **out**. I can't figure out it.	Some phrasal verbs can also be separated by a pronoun object. The pronoun cannot follow the phrasal verb.
I **ran into** my teacher/him at the mall. I ran my teacher/him into at the mall.	Some phrasal verbs cannot be separated by the object.
She **grew up** fast. The plane **took off** ten minutes late.	Some phrasal verbs have no object.

Common phrasal verbs	
Come on, let's go!	*Come on* is one of the most common phrasal verbs used in conversation.
I **get up** (= arise) early every morning. You should **look** it **up** (= search and find) online. It's not true. He **made** the story **up** (= created).	They **found out** (= discovered) my password. What's **going on** (= happening)? I **took off** (= removed) the red cap and **put on** (= placed on the body) the blue one.

Unit 5 Being Different

Lesson A Language Link: *It* + *be* + adjective + infinitive; gerund as subject

It's nice to see you again. **It's not necessary to speak** perfect English.	We often start a sentence with *it* followed by *be* + an adjective + an infinitive (*to* + verb).
Smoking is bad for your health. To smoke is bad for your health. (not common)	It's also common to start a sentence with the gerund (*-ing* form).
Mastering English grammar is challenging. **Flying** costs more than driving.	The gerund acts as a noun and is followed by the third-person singular verb form.
It's customary to tip twenty percent. = **Tipping** twenty percent **is customary**.	Sometimes ideas can be written both ways without a change in meaning.

Lesson B Language Link: Future time clauses

He's **going to have** a big party when he **graduates**. When he **graduates**, he's **going to have** a big party.		Future time clauses show two events in the future.
main clause I'**ll move out**	*time clause* as soon as I **start** college.	The main clause uses a future verb form. The time clause is usually in the simple present.
I'**ll call** him We'**re going to buy** a car	<u>after</u> **I get up** in the morning. <u>when</u> we **get married**.	In these examples, the event in the <u>time clause</u> happens first.
We'**ll start** the meeting	<u>as soon as</u> he **arrives**.	*Once/as soon as* = "right after."
I'**ll give** you my email address	<u>before</u> I **leave**.	In this sentence, the event in the <u>main clause</u> happens first.

Unit 6 Big Business

Lesson A Language Link: The passive: simple present and simple past

Active: The city closed that restaurant. *Passive:* That restaurant **was closed** (by the city).	There are often two ways to talk about an action.
Active: The police stopped <u>her</u> for speeding. *Passive:* <u>She</u> **was stopped** (by the police) for speeding.	To form the passive, use a form of *be* + the past participle. In the passive, the object becomes the subject.
The "Fallingwater" house **was built** by Frank Lloyd Wright.	Use *by* + noun to show the performer of the action.
I'**m paid** twice a month. (I know who pays my salary.) All of the money **was stolen**. (We don't know who did it.) Portuguese **is spoken** in Brazil. (Everyone speaks it.)	We don't use *by* + noun when the performer is understood, unknown, or an action is done by people in general.
Once a week, her entire house **is cleaned**. (We don't care who does it. The action is more important.)	The passive focuses on the action more than the performer.
Passive: All of the money **was stolen**. *Active:* <u>Someone</u> stole all of the money.	Use *someone/some people* when the performer's identity is unknown.

Verbs commonly used in the passive	
My parents **were born** in 1970. That song **was** originally **done** by Kanye.	Oktoberfest **is held** in Munich every year. That purse **was made** in Africa.

Lesson B Language Link: Connecting words: *because, so, although / even though*

main clause We stayed home I finished my work	*adverbial clause* **because** it was snowing. **so** I left early.	The connecting words *because, so,* and *although/even though* show the relationship in meaning between two clauses.
I got scared **because** I was lost. **Because** I was lost, I got scared.	Use *because* to give a reason for something. Notice that *because* can also start a sentence.
The traffic was terrible, **so** we missed our flight.	Use *so* to show a result.
She went to work, **even though** she was sick. **Although** she was sick, she went to work anyway.	Use *although/even though* to show surprise at the statement in the main clause.

Unit 7 Health

Lesson A Language Link: Verb + noun / adjective / verb(-*ing*); noun + *hurt(s)*

I **can't stop thinking** about the accident. I had a cold. I **couldn't stop sneezing**.	Use *can't stop + -ing* verb for repeated actions that you have no control over.
I **have a stomachache** and I **feel nauseous**. I **hurt my back** while I was exercising.	Use *have* + noun, *feel/be* + adjective, and *hurt(s)* to talk about pain.

Lesson B Language Link: Reported speech: requests and commands

The doctor said, "Get some rest."	Quoted speech uses a person's exact words. Use the verb *say* and quotation marks.
The doctor **told** <u>me</u> **to get** some rest.	Reported speech is used to report what someone else has said (but not the exact words).
The doctor **told** <u>us</u> **not to worry** about the baby.	Use *tell* in reported commands followed by an object and the infinitive.
She said, "Please turn off your cell phones." She **asked** <u>the man</u> **to turn off** his cell phone.	Use *ask* in reported requests followed by an object and the infinitive.

Unit 8 Sports and Hobbies

Lesson A **Language Link:** The present perfect (PP) vs. the present perfect continuous (PPC)

The present perfect continuous					Contractions
Subject	*Has / Have*	*Been*	**Verb + *-ing***		I've, he's, they've
She	has	been	sleeping	a lot.	

I**'ve written** my speech and I'm ready to present it.	Use the PP for an action that was started and completed in the past (specific time not stated).
I**'ve been writing** my speech. I'm not sure how to end it.	Use the PPC for an action that started in the past and continues up to now (it's not completed).
He**'s run** in a marathon twice. ~~He's been running in a marathon twice.~~	Use the PP for an action that happened on a specific number of occasions.
I**'ve known** her a long time. ~~I've been knowing her for a long time.~~	Use the PP with stative verbs (*know, belong, own, etc*).
I**'ve studied** all day. = I**'ve been studying** all day.	Use either tense with *for, all,* and *since* (and verbs like *study, live,* and *work*) with no change in meaning.

Lesson B **Language Link:** The simple past tense vs. the perfect tenses

The simple past *(I played)*	
I **visited** South Africa in 2010. I **lived** in Rome for five years. Now I live in Rio. She **finished** her homework last night.	• Use the SP for completed actions with no connection to the present. • Notice the use of past time expressions.
The present perfect *(I've played)*	
I**'ve visited** South Africa once and hope to go again. She**'s lived** in Mexico City for many years. She must love it there.	• Use the PP for completed actions when the time they happened isn't mentioned. • Use the PP for actions that started in the past and continue up to now (often with *for* and *since*).
The present perfect continuous *(I've been playing)*	
I**'ve been visiting** my friend in South Africa. I'm going home next week. He**'s been living** with us while his apartment is being painted.	• Use the PPC to talk about ongoing actions that started in the past, and continue up to now. • The PPC can also emphasize that a situation is temporary.

Unit 9 Social Issues

Lesson A Language Link: *Too* and *enough*

You're only 20. You're **too young** to vote. Actually I'm 21, so I'm **old enough** to vote.	Use *too* for amounts that are more than necessary. Use *enough* for amounts that are sufficient.
It's **too dark** in here. It's **not bright enough**. He ran **fast enough** to win the race.	*Too* comes before and *enough* comes after adjectives and adverbs.
old enough to vote / **too young** to drive	Notice the use of the infinitive.
Don't bring **too much** water. There are **too many** cars on the road.	*Too much* comes before noncount nouns, and *too many* comes before plural count nouns.
I have **too little** time to blog. There are **too few** new jobs.	*Too little* is the opposite of *too much*. *Too few* is the opposite of *too many*.

Lesson B Language Link: Future real conditionals

if clause	result clause	
If it rains,	I**'ll give** you a ride.	Future real conditionals talk about possible events in the future.
If I **hear** any news,	I**'ll call** you right away.	The verb in the *if* clause is in the simple present. The verb in the result clause takes a future form.
If the computer **overheats**,	**turn** it **off** for a while.	An imperative gives instructions or advice.
If you **press** this button,	it **ejects** the DVD.	You can also use the simple present in both clauses to state facts.

Unit 10 Having It All

Lesson A Language Link: *Wish*-statements

Currently I live in the suburbs. I **wish** I lived in the city.	Use the past tense with *wish* to talk about situations that are not true now.
I **wish** (that) I could speak English fluently.	Use *could* + base form of the verb with *wish*. *That* is optional in these sentences.
I **wish** (that) I were taller.	Use *were* for all forms of be (not was).
I can't speak French. I **wish** I could. I don't live in the city. I **wish** I did.	We often shorten *wish*-statements in this way.

Lesson B **Language Link:** Negative modals

That **couldn't** be John in the conference room. He's on vacation this week.	Use *couldn't* to say something is impossible. It carries a tone of surprise.
I **don't have to** wear a uniform. You **don't need to** know HTML to do this job.	Use *don't have to* and *don't need to* to say that something isn't necessary. You have a choice.
Once you become a member, you **may not** share your password with anyone.	Use *may not* for rules—things that are not allowed. It is more common in writing.
You **shouldn't** work so hard. You probably **shouldn't** leave until noon.	Use *shouldn't* to give advice. It means "it's not a good idea." Using *probably* softens the advice.
You**'d better not** be late or you'll miss your train.	Use *had better not* to give stronger advice. It can sound like a warning.
You **shouldn't** spend too much time with negative people. (~~You'd better not spend . . .~~)	Use *shouldn't* (but not *had better not*) for advice of a general nature.
I can speak a little Japanese, but I **can't** read it.	Use *can't* to say that you don't have the ability to do something.

Unit 11   Honestly Speaking

Lesson A **Language Link:** Present unreal conditionals

if clause (not true)	*result clause (imagined result)*	
If the ATM **gave** me extra cash,	I**'d return** the money.	Present unreal conditionals talk about imagined or unreal events.
If I **had** a million dollars,	I**'d buy** a house.	The *if* clause presents a condition that is not true right now. The result clause shows the imagined result if that condition were true.
If I **heard** a strange noise,	I**'d stay** in bed.	The verb in the *if* clause is in the simple past. The verb in the result clause takes *would* + the base form of the verb.
I **wouldn't take** that job if I **were** you.		*If I were you* . . . is often used go give advice.